A Teacher's Cry:

Expose the Truth about Education Today

Lewis W. Diuguid

Bladen County Public Library
Elizabethtown, NC 28337

Universal Publishers
Boca Raton, Florida
USA • 2004

A Teacher's Cry: Expose the Truth About Education Today

Copyright © 2004 Lewis W. Diuguid
All rights reserved.

Universal Publishers
USA • 2004

ISBN: 1-58112-519-4

www.universal-publishers.com

Contents

Prologue

This huge project would not have been possible if it had not been for a small creature named Mortimer Frog. He is featured in a book by the same name that my youngest daughter, Leslie, had to read for school. I wrote about *Mortimer Frog* and Leslie in a column headlined **"Learning by Leaps and Bounds"**:

Mortimer Frog hopped into our lives about two years ago and left us forever changed.

It started in December 1993 when Leslie's first-grade teacher, Ellen Donaldson, called me at the Southland Bureau of *The Kansas City Star*. The news was not good.

Leslie, then 7, had failed a test on the book *Mortimer Frog*. The teacher called to tell me that Leslie would be held back in reading to complete the work.

Oh, no! I thought. But I thanked the teacher for calling and then shared what I knew about *Mortimer Frog*. Leslie had brought the book home once, and when I saw it at breakfast I had her read it.

She fumbled through the pages. *Mortimer Frog* then vanished until Leslie's teacher called.

The teacher made me realize that my wife, Valerie, and I had been bamboozled by Leslie. We had kept up as two parents in high-stress jobs by double-teaming Leslie and her sister, Adrianne, then 10, until Leslie got out of kindergarten.

First grade for Leslie with homework and tests created new challenges. Keeping both girls focused on schoolwork suddenly became like spinning plates on sticks two miles apart.

We'd get one girl going, and the other would slow down. We'd get the second one spinning, and the first would start to wobble.

Mortimer Frog brought that show to a crashing end. The

6

teacher called me because Valerie was nearly unreachable at her phone company job.

I couldn't let Leslie flunk *Mortimer Frog*, so I did what most good parents would do—I cut a deal. I told Leslie's teacher that if she sent *Mortimer Frog* home with Leslie over the Christmas holidays that Leslie would return it in the new year able to recite that book forward and backward and pass the test standing on her head and writing with her toes.

The teacher bought it, and that year we had "happy *Mortimer Frog* holidays." Adrianne laughed. Leslie didn't.

I still remember the book. It was about a frog that a class of kids had named Mortimer. As Mortimer grew he kept hopping out of the bigger containers the children put him in until the students finally set him free in a nearby wetland.

We read the book repeatedly with Leslie, but I made sure that she knew its real lesson. "Don't goof off, and don't leave homework at school," she said.

Mortimer taught Valerie and me an important lesson, too. As good as we were, we couldn't keep up with our kids' efforts to sidestep schoolwork and outsmart us. Mortimer Frog forced us to change.

Coincidentally, technological and workplace changes had drained the fun from Valerie's job. She wanted to quit. Mortimer Frog just said, "Do it."

So Valerie quit her job in 1994, causing nearly half of our household income to evaporate. But we manage to get by.

We don't see it as living with less as much as Mortimer Frog just sold us on investing energy that would have gone into a job into our girls' education.

Our kids get only one shot at a good education, and that takes a partnership of school and home. Valerie now is the girls' drill instructor, marching them through studies whether they say they have homework or not.

It's caused each girl's grades to bump up a full notch.

Their self-esteem also has soared just by seeing that they have earned their "A's" through hard work.

It has been wonderful and heartening to see them make such leaps. We owe it all to Leslie's first grade teacher and the incredible rebounding legs of Mortimer Frog.

Before this episode and the lessons that it taught us, my job had been to get the girls off to school in the morning. But with Valerie now a stay-at-home mom, I had the mornings free for such things as going to Washington High School. And so thanks to that frog named Mortimer, this project became possible.

Foreword

After a recent winter storm, during a snow day, I heard a local DJ on a radio station popular among young listeners lament that he was getting a lot of calls from "uncool" kids, the ones who normally never called during the week because they were in school. When school was in session, he said, he only got calls from the "cool" kids, the ones who didn't go to school.

Listening to this dangerous drivel being beamed over many miles and into many vulnerable ears, I wondered whether kids today truly felt that getting an education was "uncool." That has long been a nagging problem for many African-American and Hispanic students, and it has become a growing concern among white students. I remember having moments of hating school when I was a student, but I also remember knowing that a good education was something that was highly valued. "Is that no longer the case?" I asked myself. Indeed, is education today just so much mediocre drudgery that it deserves all the bad press it gets? And taking it one step further, should we just write off that great experiment called "public education" as a failure and concentrate—as was done centuries ago—on educating only the elite?

Besides being an editor, I am also an educator and a parent—and, in those latter capacities, a cheerleader for the concept of public education. I had answered those questions long before I asked them: No, we should not dispense with public education. No, education is not all bad. And yes, a good education is still highly valued. But had I not been convinced of those answers before reading and editing this book, I certainly would have been afterward.

Admittedly, public education is in dire straits right now. No one can deny that fact when we know that "[s]ix million students are on the verge of dropping out of high school and a quarter of high-school [sic] students read below the basic level"; when "in urban communities, 50% [of teachers] leave the profession in five years—in part due to low pay and a lack of school system support" (qtd. in Institute). This book acknowledges that there are real and severe problems in today's schools, and it highlights some of the more salient and devastating ones that influence the quality of education today. But it also gives us snapshot after snapshot of what is often blurred by our focus on the problems alone: that students and teachers today are battling and resisting those problems in order to make education work.

This book is for students. It gives young people—particularly urban students—a voice, and we should listen. They are telling us—their parents, their teachers, their communities—that they need our support in order to be successful. They are telling us that they still *want* to succeed, and that they *know* that an education is vital to reaching their goals. And they are asking us to *listen* to their concerns and their points of view, because they have many important things to say.

This book is for teachers, future teachers, and colleges of education. It gives educators in classrooms everywhere a long-overdue and well-deserved accolade. It reaches out to them, letting them know that their struggles are not unique, urging them to improve and not give up, recognizing that educating *is* a difficult task, and that that is truly a mammoth understatement. But it also shows them that their triumphs are valued and well worth the effort.

Perhaps most of all, this book is for everyday, average Americans who want schools to be first-rate. It admonishes everyone to get involved, because only if that happens will the schools be exceptional at educating all of our communities' children. We must keep our youngsters on track by giving them the support and attention they need wherever they go, literally and metaphorically. This is not just up to parents, but also a responsibility of other members of the community. We must keep our teachers who stray on track by being a presence in education, taking a seat in the classroom, volunteering to help whenever needed long before being asked, and moving tasks inside and outside the classroom toward high-level achievement and excellence. We must make sure that government officials understand just how important we all know the education of our youth is for the future of our community and this country.

But this book is also for journalists and students of journalism. It demonstrates that more than sound-bite coverage is sometimes needed to get to the meat of an issue, to explore further, to probe deeper, to give the kind of picture the public deserves or wants. It shows a different, long-term, enlightening approach to journalism, an approach that can give important insights that otherwise might go undiscovered.

I have been close to this book for about a year now, becoming intimately familiar with those insights, carrying bits and pieces of information or text around with me in my bag or in my head. Even when I wasn't actively working on it, thoughts or statistics would surface in a conversation, or an article or book written by someone else would suddenly connect with what Lewis Diuguid was talking about. And—as you will read in these chapters—he talks about so very much, all of it important to the well-being of our youngsters, teachers, schools, and society.

Going back to (high) school again is not something many of us have on our list of priorities these days. Our lives are packed with work, family, and whatever "extra-curricular" activities we can manage to make time for. It was not on Lewis' to-do list either until he unexpectedly heard a cry from a teacher, until he received a dare he could not ignore. Chapter One explains in detail the events that moved him to return to school.

Lewis' columns have allowed me—as a parent and an educator—to go back vicariously and reacquaint myself with the current situation in our schools, connecting his experiences with whatever (few) tales my own children brought home each day. During the editing process his stories and analyses had me switching hats time and time again—from parent, to teacher, to editor—as he switched topics. I found myself repeatedly nodding my head, one hat morphing into another, as my parent-self saw the desperate need for the involvement that he is advocating, or my teacher-self empathized with the difficult task faced by today's educators and students. Wearing the hat of the editor, I tried to keep my other selves satisfied by making sure that Lewis' columns and discussion were presented in a way that did the wealth of work and information justice.

In journalism the same subject often returns again and again over the course of many years. As new insights surface or an old issue once again catches the public's eye, articles and commentary sprout and bloom like previous years' perennials, but with a slightly different look, angle, or patina.

Over the course of four years, Lewis created almost 100 columns about the microcosm of Washington High School and the larger reality it represents. Logically, similar topics and concerns would resurface as those four years progressed. In a microcosm the stages of life continue relentlessly, even though each new stage will vary as outside influences change. So, too, the life of a school remains fundamentally the same even as students and teachers adjust to whatever is going on outside the classroom walls. And the columns that Lewis wrote often present the recurring themes that reflect those issues, though each time with some change—perhaps slight, perhaps massive, but always significant.

In organizing the columns into a book, therefore, we discovered that a strict chronological approach wasn't possible. The reader would quickly become confused and the text would be repetitive. So we decided on the format that you see before you: the columns have been grouped by theme, so that they naturally lead to and support the conclusions Lewis draws from his experiences and observations.*

The chapters' themes include: the risks and rewards of involvement; myths and stereotypes; students' stresses and triumphs; the role of sports; education standards; and multiple approaches to teaching. Introducing the first four chapters are portraits of the four teachers who allowed Lewis to sit and participate in their classrooms. There are two additional teachers' portraits at the beginning of Chapters 6 and 8. The center of the book, Part III, is graced with 12 columns containing student portraits which reveal how the students see themselves. Most of these students and

---

* A complete list of all the columns mentioned, with their dates and titles, can be found in the Appendix.

teachers—as well as others not highlighted—appear in other parts of the book.

We had hoped to be able to include photographs of the students and teachers, so that names could be connected with faces. Unfortunately, this proved impossible. But in these pages readers will be able to create their own images of these incredible players on the stage of this four-year project.

The original project ended at graduation, but—predictably—the connection to the graduates and teachers did not. Some of the columns included were written about what has transpired during the five years since graduation. So far, then, the entire project has spanned more than nine years and includes well over 100 columns. In September 2000, in part because of this project, Lewis received the Missouri Honor Medal for Distinguished Service in Journalism, the highest lifetime achievement award given by the University of Missouri-Columbia School of Journalism.

It is a deserved tribute for a job well done, a unique approach to journalism, a unique look at education. As editor, parent, and teacher, I hope that the important information contained in this book will inspire communities across the country to not only tackle the undeniable problems from the outside but to also give students and teachers the support they need and deserve from the inside. This book shows us the way and beckons us to follow. It is up to us to take the next step.

Elsje M. Smit, Editor

Introduction

*W*ashington High School, Kansas City, Kansas. I can still see the tan brick school building at 7340 Leavenworth Road, the circular drive out front and the school buses, parents, guardians, friends and older siblings with cars dropping off teenagers of all colors for early morning classes.

I learned a lot being there and writing columns on the experience in *The Kansas City Star*. Beyond the books I have read on education, the best lessons I've received came from going back to high school. The project was a re-immersion into a world I had left behind more than 20 years earlier, in 1973, when I graduated from Southwest High School in St. Louis. I have shared some of that knowledge in more than 100 columns and many speeches to groups around the country. But none of what I wrote or presented told the complete story.

This book comes out as the Class of 1999 observes its fifth reunion. On their anniversary, what this book is meant to do is provide a more comprehensive view of the Washington High School learning experiences, so as to give parents, grandparents, aunts, uncles, taxpayers, educators, students, business people, and civic and faith leaders a new understanding of public education.

From 1995 to 1999, Washington High School became a second place of work and a home for me. The Class of 1999 started out with 439 students on Sept. 20, 1995. As often happens in urban schools with families moving, changing addresses and transferring children to other schools, the number of students in the Class of 1999 at Washington High School plunged 29 percent to 312 by Sept. 20, 1996, and fell an additional 14 percent to 269 juniors by Sept. 20, 1997. Only about 150 students in the Class of 1999 graduated. But no one records which of the students simply enrolled elsewhere and which dropped out.

Washington High School is an ethnically and racially mixed school. For example, the 1997 fall enrollment of 1,273 students was 17.98 percent white, 64.65 percent black, 11.7 percent Hispanic, 5.49 percent Asian American and 0.16 percent American Indian. As in other urban school districts, the percentage of minority students was a lot higher than the percentage of minorities in the general population.

At the time of this project, Wyandotte County had more than its share of poverty. The odd thing was the area had a lot of high paying jobs. But the people who held those jobs didn't live in that community. The U.S. Bureau of Economic Analysis data showed that the average annual wage per job in Wyandotte County was $34,388. But the average personal income of Wyandotte County residents was only $20,191—the lowest in the Kansas City metropolitan area. The gap between what's made in Wyandotte County and what stays in Wyandotte County also is the highest in the metropolitan area. To the east in Jackson County, Mo., for example, the average worker makes $35,623 compared with the average personal income of residents of $30,020. South of Wyandotte County lies Johnson County, Kan. It's where a lot of people making high salaries in Wyandotte County live and where people who live in Wyandotte County get low-paying service jobs. The average worker in Johnson County makes $36,723 compared with residents' $43,168 in average annual personal income.

Terry Woodbury, then-president of the United Way of Wyandotte County, said during an interview I had with him in 2002 that five of eight persons who work in Wyandotte County export their earnings to places like Johnson County. Those jobs are at workplaces such as the University of Kansas Medical Center, the General Motors Corp. Fairfax plant, Colgate-Palmolive Co., Procter & Gamble and Owens-Corning Fiberglas Corp. It sets up a reality of wealth being drained from the community where students such as those at Washington High School live.

They also have seen the flight of people from their community. The census shows that Wyandotte County had a population of 185,495 in 1960. It grew to 186,845 in 1970 but has been falling ever since. It was 157,882 in 2000. So this is a community that has suffered many losses. Young people are not oblivious to these types of hardships. Yet teachers have to contend with the trauma this causes as the students bring it into the schools.

15

Besides administrators, teachers and students, there are few people who know just what goes on in our schools from day to day. Although I frequently give talks to students in area schools I, too, see only the most obvious aspects of everyday school life. So when I received a dare from freshman English teacher Alice Bennett to learn what it's really like to be a teenager and teacher today, I couldn't resist being lured back to high school. The first year I attended six of Ms. Bennett's classes, trying to get to the school at least once a week and going to different classes each week. The second year she helped me get a spot in Beatrice McKindra's sophomore English classes. The third year, Bennett got American history teacher Scott Milkowart to give me a seat in his classes of juniors. Then for my final year, Bennett persuaded American government teacher Dennis Bobbitt to let me study with his seniors. The names of those teachers and of many of their students appear in the chapters that follow.

My goal was to focus at least two of the 12 columns that I then wrote per month for *The Star* on what took place with the students and teachers from day to day. I studied with the students in the classrooms, attended pep assemblies and went to after-school events. I watched the students perform in sports, the arts and music. I visited the teens at their jobs and in their homes. Even though the information and impressions I got made up only about 15 percent of the columns I wrote in those 4 years, the project consumed about 45 percent of my time. Journalism by phone and the Internet may work in many circumstances to relay news and information to readers, but it couldn't get me close enough to tell the students' and teachers' massive story about public education. I had to be there with the teens and teachers to tell of their day-to-day interactions, their lives, the challenges they faced, and their hopes and dreams, to put together a tableau of what public education does for those who work and study in our public schools.

The four-year project was unprecedented, and my columns made up what may have been the longest running series *The Star* has ever printed. But beyond the sheer volume of the project, what stands out most is how different the approach was. In journalism we normally tell people about school board elections and votes. We cover the school administration and all of its faults. We write about teachers' unions, teacher shortages, teacher incompetence and the problems teachers face in the classroom. We discuss troubled and violent children such as those who carried out the mass shootings on April 20, 1999, at Columbine High School near Littleton, Colorado. We write about low achievement scores, failed desegregation efforts, the poverty-fed sufferings of inner-city children and schools, teen pregnancies, drug and alcohol abuse and the high truancy and dropout rates. We cover the waterfront when it comes to the problems—and that has long been considered good journalism. Occasionally we write about gifted students' successes and education innovations. But we don't tell people what they crave most: what is taking place *day to day* in public schools.

One of the thunderous realities that Washington High School revealed was that the negatives about urban education *are* rooted in facts. But the positives also are starkly real, showing that teachers *do* find a way to get through to children despite the many learning obstacles. Washington High School showed me there is no simplicity in sinners and winners, no black and white—just constantly changing shades of gray.

This situation is illustrated by the many contorting contradictions about education that the following chapters in this book will illuminate. The book started as an attempt to tell the story of the Class of 1999 at Washington High School, which I followed from the students' freshman year until they graduated. But my immersion at Washington High School and the ensuing columns I wrote in *The Kansas City Star* took readers on a four-year journey into the skyscraper of education. This book, however, widens the view of education in America beyond just a compilation of those columns. Washington High School provides much-needed insight into education in America—particularly in urban areas.

The tug of war between the positive and negative experiences in urban schools helped reveal in retrospect how urban education in particular seems to have its own *multiple personality disorder*. In her book *United We Stand: A Book for People with Multiple Personalities*, Eliana Gil, Ph.D., writes that abused children sometimes "create separate and distinct personalities," or "alters" to confront difficulties that they themselves can't cope with in their lives (4). These alters have "allowed [them] to protect [themselves] and remain sane in the face of severe abuse . . . to endure the bad times and to keep [their] heart and soul safe from abusers" (21). For children it is a means of survival.

The same might be said for urban schools, which have had to find a way to survive in the face of governmental and societal abuse. Urban education, therefore, seems to have come up with several "alters" of its own. One character that has emerged is an injured personality, with much of the news about inner-city schools only showing problem children, low test scores, substandard materials, deficient teachers and administrators, high turnover, high dropout rates, poor academic performance and a perennial challenge to President George W. Bush's underfunded No Child Left Behind education mandate. Another is one that's angry and belligerent. That shows up in the behavior of too many students, parents, teachers and administrators—each reacting to how they have been bullied and mistreated. A third is one that rolls over and plays dead. This may be the most detrimental of all. Teachers and administrators who should have their doors open inviting in parents, business people and professionals are surrendering to a bunker mentality. They've become less open to having people come in, less likely to take classes on field trips, fearing embarrassment, fearing the repercussions from either misbehavior or the perception that they have nothing dynamic to show. Minimal effort at educating children is the outcome. What educators are missing are the allies they could have in their classrooms, the raised standards for behavior that outsiders import into education and the increasing amount of new material and real world experiences that parents and other adults bring to the process of educating. (See Chapter 7.)

Urban education's multiple personality disorder is created out of trauma, and our country for decades has traumatized urban schools and urban kids with slashed resources, white flight and negative media. Schools have been bullied by governments and communities, made to think that, no matter what they do, it is never enough to meet the high standards needed to become "acceptable." There is always something more that needs to be done to open that door to success. And school administrators, parents and students—under pressure to perform—have ended up bullying those who are on the front lines of learning: the teachers.

This became clear to me as I was reading a book titled *Bullies, Targets & Witnesses: Helping Children Break the Pain Chain* by SuEllen Fried and her daughter, Paula Fried, Ph.D. SuEllen Fried is a longtime friend, an advocate for nonviolence and founder of the Stop Violence Coalition based in Kansas City, Mo. She conducts seminars nationwide on the prevention of youth violence. Her book takes a head-on look at the causes and prevention of bullying as a way to curtail greater acts of violence such as shootings in our post-Columbine High School society. But contained in the message the Frieds are conveying is the fact that this country, its parents and children for years have increasingly been bullying teachers. The book defines such abuse as "emotional bullying" (58), as opposed to the other three types—physical, verbal and sexual bullying. "The concept of emotional bullying is the most challenging of the four types to transmit," the Frieds write (61). They go on to explain that

> [t]here are two categories of emotional bullying: nonverbal and psychological. Nonverbal emotional bullying is pointing, staring, mugging. Laughing, rolling your eyes, making faces, sticking out your tongue, writing notes, drawing pictures, flicking people off, using the third finger or a number of other hand signals that imply "loser," "crazy," or irreverent and sexual innuendos. Psychological emotional bullying comes in the form of indirect abuse such as exclusion, isolation, rejection, turning your back on someone when they try to talk with you, shunning, ostracizing, and ignoring. It may be subtle, or it may be overt.... I often tell children that when someone commits a crime in our society, we send them to prison. Prison officials had to come up with something worse than incarceration for those who break a law while they are jailed, so they created solitary confinement. One of the cruelest forms of punishment that humans can inflict on one

another is total isolation. Prisoners of war who have been physically tortured and isolated state that the isolation is at least as bad, if not worse, than the physical torture.... It appears that the places in our society where isolation is most likely to happen are prisons and playgrounds! (58-59)

Teachers feel that isolation as they are bullied by students, bullied by parents, bullied by administrators, and bullied by federal, state and local governments in being required to do more while given no funding or extra help to accomplish each new impossible task. The No Child Left Behind mandate is a perfect example of what's being done to teachers and the budgetary, professional and emotional trauma that it is causing. Then Secretary of Education Rod Paige made matters worse on Feb. 23, 2004, when he told a meeting of the nation's governors in Washington, D.C., that the largest teachers' union was a "terrorist organization" for not supporting the No Child Left Behind Act. Reg Weaver, president of the 2.7 million member National Education Association, denounced Paige for making that remark. Paige later apologized ("Education secretary"). But what he said was unforgivable particularly when the United States is embroiled in an unending war against terrorism after the Sept. 11, 2001, attacks in which commercial airlines were hijacked and flown like missiles into the World Trade Center in New York City and the Pentagon in Washington, D.C. Paige's off-color remark brands teachers as enemies and makes efforts to educate our children seem like a war in which teachers are the "evil" and "evil-doers," which Bush and others in his administration have labeled terrorists. But teachers aren't evil. They're not evil-doers, and they're not our enemy. Teachers are our children's unsung heroes, and they need to be recognized as such. However, they are publicly damned by people from Paige on down to parents when things go wrong. We have placed teachers in impossible situations and then we blame them for being there.

Incredibly, teachers have been absorbing the punishing emotional bullying. But they can't keep taking it forever. The Frieds write that Americans "need to know that if they inflict pain on someone, it does not evaporate; it does not disappear—most likely it collects. When enough pain has collected in a person's soul, it can turn to rage" (65). Again, that's about children's anguish over being bullied, but it applies to teachers as well. The Frieds quote Dr. Karl Menninger, a famed Kansas psychiatrist, who "states that children, like adults, develop behavior patterns that allow them to survive" (123).

Keep in mind that teachers are only human, too, and they respond to ill-treatment just as anyone else in any other profession would. As the Frieds point out, "[w]hen a child's basic security is not threatened, he or she is free to pursue higher goals; when he or she is under siege, he or she will resort to life-preserving actions. In his book *The Human Mind*, Dr. Menninger writes: 'When a trout, rising to a fly gets hooked on a line and finds himself unable to swim about freely, he begins a fight which results in struggles and splashes and sometimes an escape. Often, of course, the situation is too tough for him. In the same way, the human being struggles with his environment and with the hooks that catch him. Sometimes he masters his difficulties; sometimes they are too much for him. His struggles are all that the world sees and it usually misunderstands them. It is hard for a free fish to understand what is happening to a hooked one'" (123-124).

Teachers—suffering severe emotional bullying—are those hooked fish. Sometimes they strike out in response to how they've been treated and the lack of support that they receive, and our children pay the price, receiving a poor education or worse, as this book will in some ways describe. Yet, *as caring professionals many struggle against being bullied to try to do a good job teaching kids whom many in our society have cast off as losses.*

A fourth character of urban schools that I've noted from the Washington High School project, then, is the one that illustrates this effort on the teachers' part: it is the *survivor achieving*, though lost in the struggle, with the other personalities getting all the public attention. And in this book I have tried to highlight this "survivor." In pointing out that education in this country is not "all good" or "all bad," but that what happens in the schools slides between those extremes and can therefore be hard to grasp for people on the outside, I have tried to give a multifaceted view of today's schools showing that, despite the difficulties, they are mostly good.

People I have met over the years have said that this Washington High School project opened a window for them into that sky-scraper of public education: they could see what went on inside the superstructure of public schools. The series gave them a better understanding of what educators and children were doing. It helped them to ask more informed questions about schools and to get better answers. For them, Washington High School became a microcosm for education. I hope that the knowledge and impressions collected in this book will open similar windows for many more, showing that teachers still teach and children still learn, even as they contend with the often daunting modern-day challenges of public education.

But the schools' multiple personality disorder is a mental health concern that needs constant treatment from the community. People in communities across America need to do more, to get involved and stay active in our schools. The Frieds in their book on bullying say witnesses to such abuse of children have an enormous power to stop such non-verbal violence in its tracks. They do it in the support that they give to the target of the bullying, in challenging the bully and in notifying an adult so the bullying ends. Adults need to be the same sort of advocates for schools and teachers, providing assistance in the classroom, going to bat for teachers against unjust criticism and advocating for more government funding for teachers and education.

My friend, Mahnaz Shabbir, includes in her speeches about Muslim women and the need for a lasting peace this quote from Mohandas Gandhi: "We are the change we wish to see in the world." Parents and adults in neighborhoods surrounding all schools must be the change they wish to see in the education of all children.

Outsiders also need to insist that schools maintain high standards to better serve the community. But all of those many roles need to work together, making the schools and the people in them the centerpiece of the neighborhoods they serve. And government policy toward public school funding can change if enough people speaking on behalf of teachers and students insist that it happen. Teachers are the best champions our children have and we must give them a fighting chance to do their jobs.

Part I
Chapter 1
The Challenge

Listen to teachers. Listen closely. What they have to say, will affect the education and well-being of our children and our community.

PORTRAIT:
Alice Bennett

Urban schools seemed to hold both an irresistible challenge and a heartache for Alice Bennett. Those conflicting feelings prompted her to send me her emotion-laden letters and to subsequently open her classroom to me. Those feelings for urban school kids also gave her the courage to do what many teachers wouldn't: to risk having a columnist in her classes, taking notes and writing about everyday occurrences at Washington High School. But her courage started long before I got to know her.

Bennett's teaching career began in a most atypical way. She is from Wichita, Kan., where she finished her senior year in high school. Then she and her mother moved to the Kansas City area to join her father who had taken a job in this community. Bennett's route to college and teaching, however, was circuitous. She said she did the traditional white, middle-class thing, going to college immediately after graduating from high school. But Bennett flunked out, not once, but twice—first after her freshman year at Baker University in Baldwin City, Kan., and then the following year as a freshman at Central Missouri State University in Warrensburg, Mo. Afterward, Bennett was hired at WDAF-AM radio and later she moved to WHB-AM, doing secretarial work. She said she had a lot of fun

Bladen County Public Library
Elizabethtown, NC 28337

planning promotions, working with the DJs and other personalities.

"The DJs are crazy people," Bennett recalled. "At some level it was glamorous. But it wasn't enough."

Bennett returned to Central Missouri State University and worked as a secretary at the old Kansas City General Hospital to earn money to help put herself through college. By this time, she knew she wanted to be a teacher. "I felt that I liked working with kids," Bennett said. "I felt I had something to offer, and because I had such a different route [in completing my education] I felt I had something to relate."

Although Bennett was working, she found that she still had to depend on the government commodities food program, the precursor to food stamps. She also earned money by doing public relations work for the university museum. "I'd write news releases, take pictures and make sure they'd get in the local papers," Bennett said.

At Central Missouri State University, Bennett received her bachelor of science degree in education in 1974 and her master of arts in communications in 1981. Her non-traditional path continued from there. When she neared her graduation, she realized that she had a better chance of getting a job at an urban school instead of a suburban school, where most of her classmates did their student teaching. That led her to student-teach in an inner-city school, which dismayed university officials.

She went to Lincoln High School, where the principal said it was the first time in 20 years that a white female teacher out of college had been placed there. Bennett stayed at Lincoln High School two years. She married the physical education teacher at Lincoln High School after she had left the district to take other journalism jobs. They have a son, Brad. Bennett later returned to teaching, taking a job in the Kansas City, Kan., School District.

I never thought her family was any different from other families until one day in her first-hour freshman English class. Her students and I were talking about vacations, places where we'd been and where we would like to go. Bennett, who was busy in another part of the room, got into the conversation saying she and her then-husband had been to the Caribbean and enjoyed the experience. She added, however, that the people on the island had treated her husband different than they'd treated her. She remembered that people expressed more of a recognition, intimacy and rapport with her husband. The students and I said that perhaps it was because they deferred to men. "No," Bennett responded. "It's because my husband is black." Bennett's students and I looked at each other with amazement. It was the first time she had shared that information. It was the first instance in which that aspect of Bennett's private life had a reason to come forward. It surprised us and at the same time it gave us greater insight into, and more respect and admiration for, someone who cared about the students and the work she did as a teacher.

After two years at Lincoln and a stint at Northwest Middle School in Kansas City, Kan., Bennett started teaching at Washington High School. She's been there for 23 years, teaching journalism until 1993, and serving as the yearbook and newspaper adviser. When she and I met, Bennett was teaching in the language arts department. She's now back to teaching journalism full-time.

Bennett says educators must have people skills, a sense of humor and courage to get lessons across to students. But she also maintains that teachers must "have the courage to stand up to [the] administration and say, 'No, this child does not meet the standards.'"

Teachers like Bennett make a difference. I witnessed that at Washington High School.

But beyond her bold actions in her academic and professional careers, she has also shown great courage in her personal life. Bennett never made an issue of her health, but she is a cancer survivor. When we talked just about her in January 2000 she had trouble remembering years and dates such as when she received her diplomas. But she was quick to recall that Dec. 21, 1998, marked the fifth year that her cancer had been in remission. She had been diagnosed the first part of December 1993. Surgery followed on Dec. 21, 1993, with radiation for five weeks.

She never let on what she had suffered and overcome when I got to know her at Washington High School. But a mutual friend told me.

Such things are good to know. At school Bennett and I chatted about things large and small involving her classes, her expectations, her students, their parents and the community. At times we'd shift gears completely and talk about our weekend plans, our spouses, our children and the dreams we had for our families. It helped each of us to see the human side of the other and to care about the task we had to perform and our well-being on a personal level.

We made a habit of having lunch each summer after I had started at Washington High School. It was just to continue the good conversations. I also felt honored when I asked and she accepted the challenge to talk about Washington High School with me to a few groups that were eager to hear about the project beyond what they had read in the newspaper. I often went solo on such speaking engagements. But Bennett added great depth to the discussions. She even appeared with me on "The Walt Bodine Show," a Kansas City radio talk show, in the spring of 1996 after "our" students had finished their freshman year.

Bennett is an exceptionally good educator and communicator for the school district and the teaching profession. She's also a great mother and friend. I never had a chance to say all of that in a column for *The Kansas City Star*. I'm glad that this book has given me that opportunity.

*M*any good things begin in disjointed ways. My involvement at Washington High School was no exception. It started on May 31, 1995. That day, I received a letter from a suburban teacher whose class I had visited in 1993. That day, a column I had written about my experiences at a school in her district prompted the teacher to write.

The column ran in *The Kansas City Star* under the headline, **"Today's youth could benefit from a slow-motion setting"**:

A bell blared, and the classroom thundered with expensive sneakers stampeding for the door.

The young herd left embarrassment, disgust and frustration on the suburban high school counselor's face. She had asked me to talk to the students about journalism but didn't like that I had to nearly stand on my head and verbally turn some of them on their noggins to get and keep their attention.

"I'm sorry for what you had to go through," she said. "Our kids today are just overstimulated."

I thought about that a lot and then called the counselor later to get her to elaborate. She did but asked that her name and school not be used to keep people from turning on her for telling the truth.

I'll preface what she told me by saying that the majority of today's youths are good. But more than in the past, many share a problem that the counselor exposed with a simple question: "Have you ever noticed that our kids are seemingly in steady motion?

"They think action all the time. They think the only means of function is motion."

I call it the Mountain Dew syndrome. On television, soft-drink ads preach the rush of super-action fueled by a sugar high as the only way to live.

Children plug in to that media power surge for more

hours than they spend in school and develop a voracious appetite for it. TV, movies, computer games, videos, music and other media keep them so pumped up that they become addicted to the roar and can't unplug the buzz—even in school.

"They need to be entertained in the classroom rather than calmly sitting, listening and learning," said the counselor, who as an educator for more than 30 years has worked at a community college, a university, and elementary, junior high and high schools. "It affects how they take in information."

Abstract and reasoning skills suffer because students can't plow deep into still, reflective waters of thought. Henry David Thoreau would have to be a hip-hop rapper or throw a loud electric guitar into Walden Pond to get kids' attention today.

"We're just in a noisier world," the counselor said. Teens today are affected more than in the past as passive consumers of the hype.

As a result, the counselor said, course work doesn't get covered because teachers must contend with disruptions and short attention spans. Communication skills also have eroded.

Hallways fill with sound bites and happy talk. "It's a kind of senseless motion, too," she said.

Many kids don't read, and writing isn't in vogue. Their problem-solving skills also have suffered.

"They feel so powerless over everything," she said. "When a problem comes up, they say, 'Let me call my mother.'

"They have been raised to be dependent."

They're like windup toys without direction. But kids aren't toys. They're people who eventually must join and compete with everyone else in the work force.

But the counselor said many parents gum up the transition by bankrolling kids' addiction for fun and screaming louder than young people do when told that students must do homework. It's easier for adults to not get involved.

That feeds what I call a cycle of blame. Industries indict colleges, which fault high schools. High schools dump on middle schools, which then point fingers at elementary schools for sending them ill-prepared students.

"But I think people will have to face the truth," the counselor said.

Deborah Prothrow-Stith, an assistant dean at the Harvard School of Public Health, spoke "the truth" at a forum last year. She said our kids consume our time, attention, money and other resources, whether we choose to give it to them in a wholesome way or they take it from us when they're in a crisis.

Replacing the hype now with quiet, studious environments that promote learning is a start. It may save us from tragedies that no one wants later.

The follow-up letter from the teacher whose classroom I had visited $2^1/_2$ years earlier carried its own plaintive message. She wrote:

Like the school counselor in today's paper, you visited my classroom several years ago on a happier note. My students wrote about random acts of kindness and you honored their written work and noble deeds by publishing them in a holiday edition. I have been very negligent in thanking you but want to make sure you know how much your visit meant. *Because this is my last school year*, I feel especially responsible to encourage caring consistent modeling, prodding and nurturing. Please keep writing about kids and visiting schools whenever possible.

Thanks once again for your contribution to our community in words and actions.

P.S. Attached and enclosed is a copy of our family newsletter that I publish with my explanation about quitting teaching. I thought you might be interested. Feel free to use any ideas if you like but not my name as I need to protect my students' identity.

The column and student essays the teacher spoke of had run in *The Kansas City Star* on Dec. 23, 1993. It chronicled the upbeat, innovative work that the teacher was doing to get the students to treat people better, particularly during the holiday season. It made her letter and explanation about her leaving the teaching profession all the more tragic.

In journalism, timing is everything. I thought that what her 1995 correspondence offered would stand out best at the start of the new school year. I wrote her back promising to call her at the end of summer. The following column resulted from the teacher's earlier letter and our subsequent conversation. It ran in September under the headline, **"Teaching career lost its spark"**:

A suburban teacher's letter made me wonder what went wrong.

Two years ago I watched her work wonders with students. But the 42-year-old teacher's recent correspondence said she was calling it quits.

Teaching had become a battle, and she couldn't answer the bell when it rang in another school year this week.

"The career that I once so much enjoyed, I now, at best, merely endured," she wrote. "When the job satisfaction was gone, the regular paycheck and job security kept me hanging on."

But classroom tragedies made her "fully aware I had been prostituting myself too long." One of her students became pregnant, another was shot and paralyzed and she was falsely accused of abuse.

When I called her during her summer of healing, she

31

gave me a tough assignment: Find an instructional way to tell what happened so that kids will learn; parents, administrators and the community will be supportive; and suffering teachers will keep the spark that she lost when she flamed out.

"I know I sound pretty burned out, but I've also heard that people can't burn out unless they were once on fire," said the teacher, who asked that her name not be used. "And I was on fire once in my career."

The teacher roared into her first job with a college degree at age 21.

"I remember early on almost being surprised that they were paying me for this because I enjoyed it so much," she said. "Teaching school, having your own classroom is kind of like being your own boss, having your own business."

She could teach children, and they would achieve wonderful things.

"I loved kids, and I loved learning myself," said the teacher, who has a master's degree and has taught in elementary, middle and high school and special education. "Teaching was an excuse to be a career student myself.

"It was a fun way to learn and to pass it on to other people. In the past few years I was doing precious little of that.

"I was a single parent to about 100 kids every day, and it was overwhelming."

Many kids aren't on fire with learning, either. They've got adult problems. Many are from single-parent homes and worry about food, clothing, violence, peer pressure, alcohol, drugs and teen pregnancy.

"You try to pass on a certain amount of guidance, serenity and hope to your kids—that life is going to get better," the teacher said. "And yet for me as a caretaker, I felt like I was being drained."

Teachers spend their days as cops, nurses and parents. They are counselors to the kids and to parents when they fight at school conferences. Parents also rarely back teachers when it comes to homework and discipline.

Administrators cave in, too, fearing lawsuits and other fallout. Yet, many insist on paperwork and pleasing state regulators with high standardized test scores with regurgitated student responses.

Teachers feel isolated with parents' and administrators' doors closed. Little teaching occurs, and class sizes have risen when they should be dropping.

Simply put, the dysfunctional virus in families has bled into schools, and unless it's stopped businesses will catch it next. My friend, the teacher, had the option of picking another career.

We don't have the luxury of selecting another society. We have to make this one better.

It starts at home. We need to keep many sparks going so that no one flames out on our teachers, schools and kids.

That column prompted Alice Bennett, an English teacher at Washington High School in Kansas City, Kan., to send me two long tearful letters. One was dated Sept. 26, 1995; the other Sept. 27, 1995. In both, Bennett essentially wondered how that suburban teacher dared say she couldn't take it anymore. She wouldn't know what "taking it" was like until she had worked in an urban school district. What follows are parts of Bennett's first three-page letter:

It is with this anger that I now write to you—and, at this time, I cannot define any plausible reason why I should be doing so. So the poor little suburban teacher just found the obstacles too hard to surmount on a daily basis, year by year. Lady, as an inner-city high school teacher in Kansas City, Kan., I suffered burnout years ago. Now I suffer daily abuse that the average citizen would find appalling.

How I wish I could just walk away from my classroom. But, please, do not misunderstand the direction this written whatever is taking. I cannot walk away not because of some God-given desire to continually lay my mental, emotional and sometimes physical self on the line to help these so-called deprived students of today.

No, I cannot just leave my classroom, or my school, or my district for that matter, because I have no real options open to me. After 16 years in this district, I can afford neither to leave nor to go to another one. (I would, at most, as a teacher, receive approximately seven years credit on the pay scale transferring to another district in the state of Kansas.) If I transfer out of my building, I lose my seniority in a district that has done nothing but cut back on teaching positions for the past 10 years. And, if I get out of teaching, the best corporate position I could probably hope for would be an entry level position, if a corporation would hire a 51-year-old former secretary, journalism/English teacher.

...I'm stuck and at the end of another day of abuse as a public schoolteacher all I want to do is take a shower to wash away the filth—a situation not unlike one of a rape victim.

There have been times I have toyed with the notion of talking with a *Star* reporter or editor to encourage them to "enroll" a reporter in our school so they may report on the chaos that is our daily schedule. But then reality sets in, and no one in their right mind wants to come to work where, at 7:00 in the morning, as the students are getting off their buses, it's "motherfucker" this and "motherfucker" that. No one understands, or cares, what the big deal is when a teacher asks a student to wait at the end of the hall until the admitting bell rings before they go to their locker—and students do not hesitate one millisecond to cuss the teacher out. Good morning to you, too!

I was staggered by the despair in Bennett's letters and wondered how that perpetual fall from feeling empowered and charged up as a teacher might affect her personally. And what about her students, I asked myself, who likely sensed how she felt about them. How were these teenagers affected?

Bennett's letters went on to say how some students rarely attended class. Others arrived late, and many came without the necessary books or supplies for learning. Some students roamed the hallways "knowing nothing will be done about it, knowing they can cuss a teacher out and may or may not be given an office detention if any action is taken at all, feel free to bring dope, alcohol and guns on school premises (even though we are supposed to be a drug free, etc., zone) because nothing will be done about it." She continued:

> Yes, I have had a student who was removed from my room for a day because he had a gun in his book bag. Just last year, three students were caught in my room selling dope. Two of them were back in school within two weeks—although told by either an administrator or counselor not to go to my class, so they just roamed the building. The third student who was 18 was simply expelled. No criminal charges were ever brought against these three black male students. Students who are finally given OSS, out of school suspension, repeatedly roam our halls—why not? That's where their friends are, the dope is, it's warm, safe (who's going to stop you?) and you probably have a lunch ticket, so you can get a free lunch! Beats staying out on the street, huh? Of course going to class to learn something is out of the question.

> Every juvenile judge feels compelled to put criminal offenders back into the public school classroom.

It certainly was pleasant last year when I had the girl with the ankle monitor in my class. I can't begin to tell you how many students (unfortunately many black males) are on probation. Apparently the deal is they have to be in school—the judge doesn't stop to consider that they don't want to be here, are disruptive and often violent, resulting in their not learning anything or any other student for that matter.

Bennett made it sound as if the schools were under siege in a war, in which kids parachute in as troops unprepared for the tough duty of learning, and teachers are platoon leaders who go home each workday suffering post-traumatic stress disorder in the losing battle to educate our children. It goes back to what the Frieds described in their book, *Bullies, Targets & Witnesses: Helping Children Break the Pain Chain,* as the fish on the hook syndrome—teachers struggling against the difficulties they encounter every day as they try to resist the feeling that the battle might already be lost.

The Frieds provide some statistics on what teachers actually have to face:

In "Violence in American Schools," the authors report that in 1999, the odds of dying a violent death in school were 1 in 2 million. Yet, for the school year 1996-97, the U.S. Department of Education reported 188,000 fights or physical attacks not involving weapons in schools, 11,000 fights involving weapons, and 4,000 incidents of sexual assault. In addition, a Department of Education report covering the school year 1997-98, states that 1.3 percent of 2,752 murders of youths aged 5 through 19 took place in schools. Schools were the setting for 31 percent of 802,900 serious violent crimes against students, aged 12 to 18. Violent crimes are defined as rape, sexual assault, robbery and aggravated assault (10-11).

Teachers as human beings are affected by this. But if this isn't already bad enough, it gets worse, as Bennett described in her letters: the teachers themselves are also direct victims of the violence. The Frieds write: "According to a study conducted by the National Education Association, 6,250 teachers are threatened with bodily injury *on a daily basis* [emphasis added], and 260 are physically attacked. In an average month in public secondary schools, 5,000 teachers are actually harmed. In one week in 1995, three teachers died as a result of bullying. Two were killed outright by students, and a third teacher died of a heart attack while being assaulted...." The authors add that Richard M. Ingersoll, a researcher at the University of Pennsylvania, analyzed the federal schools and staffing survey data from more than 50,000 teachers and found that "29 percent of teachers leave the field after three years on the job and 39 percent leave within five years.... While the average annual turnover rate in most other professions is 11 percent, teachers leave theirs at a rate of 13.2 percent a year.... Their dreams of educating young people about history, science, math, literature, language, and social studies are often shattered by the reality of the disruptive classroom" (11-12).

That makes me ask the question: what's happening at home? The parents, like the people of the United States in the Vietnam War, are a fractured, unsupportive lot. On the one hand people are saying the schools have gone to hell and the kids are all bad. On the other hand adults are shouting that the students should be coddled more to protect their self-esteem and that it's the educator's fault that everything is so incredibly wrong. Then, especially in our urban schools, there is abandonment of funds and families partly because of racism and classism and partly because those institutions of learning have gotten an undeserved reputation of being the worst places to educate kids.

Bennett also was disturbed by age or social promotions. Teachers in lower grades advanced kids to the next grade whether those students had achieved passing marks or not:

> Last year 66 students in USD 500 (the Kansas City, Kan., School District) were transferred out of the middle schools to high schools without one single passing grade. It's known as age promotion.

37

Has a nice ring to it doesn't it? I have had two separate students who have been placed in my class and have never done one lick of work—or intend to. Hey, why should they? They got this far didn't they and with just a little more perseverance, they have a couple of years of being with their friends before they get bored or pregnant or arrested or leave.

Tell me, little miss suburban schoolteacher, have you ever walked by a group of students who, just as you are past, spitefully, quietly say "bitch"— knowing they are perfectly safe in doing so? Tell me little miss suburban schoolteacher what kind of bizarre behavior problems or non-existent reading levels did you have to deal with in every class, every day, every year!

Bennett went on to talk about school administrators who were unsupportive and whose actions resulted in new teachers abandoning the district. "Please understand, Mr. Diuguid, it is now 11:00 p.m. (past my bedtime, 5:00 a.m. comes very early), and I have written most of this whatever through tears. I don't know why I wrote or what I expect from you. I just know I had to do it."

In her second letter, which was six pages long, Bennett added more information and brought up more concerns. The letter told of her accomplishments as a teacher, school newspaper and yearbook adviser. Then she lamented the diminishing standards in education in public schools, the dwindling support from parents and administrators, and the rise in problems pouring through school doors from the streets of the inner city. She told of verbal and physical attacks on teachers, students caught having sex in the auditorium during school time, fights among students, teachers showing R-rated movies in class to keep students' attention, and overcrowded classrooms.

How does a school system justify setting no standards or expectations on students—regardless of who they are? Our students pay no book fee. Our students do not have to purchase a gym suit. Our students do not have to pass any classes to be promoted. Our students do not have to bring books, pencils or paper to class. There is no consequence. Our students only have to pass one quarter in order to pass a year-long class. Our students only have to pass four subjects in order to be eligible to play sports. Our students do not have to be able to read or write or do math at their appropriate level in order to pass.... I do not understand ignorance and a system that allows it to be perpetuated!

Bennett also was distressed by the school system that pulled the best and brightest students away from the rest, enrolled them in Sumner Academy, where they achieved phenomenal success without being held back by problem students' low achievement. However, students at Washington High and the other schools then suffered because academic competition became less intense. Students aren't kicked out, but they have low expectations for academic achievement. They're also permitted to have bad attitudes and use foul language and even smoke pot during a school sponsored homecoming pep rally, Bennett wrote in her second letter.

With a system in place that guarantees failure and ensures minimum effort at best, I refuse to get too excited about this or to take the blame. Me, I'm trapped. It's just eight years until I could realistically retire. But who's counting?

Once again, Mr. Diuguid, it is very late. Somewhere in all this I believe there is a series of Pulitzer Prize winning newspaper stories. More than one successful book has been published talking about such problems. Try *Savage Inequalities* [by Jonathan Kozol]. Maybe through all my tiredness, frustration, anger (and possibly prejudice) I'm looking for some validation that these inequities need to be told. Told by me, by you, by someone.???

Good night, Mr. Diuguid. I hope your two lovely

daughters never have to grace the threshold of Washington High School.

I wrote Bennett back, thanking her for the letters and letting her know that I was moved by the many things she had written. I apologized for the daily tragedies she had to endure in our flawed system of educating children. I shared with her the similar frustrations my dad, Dr. Lincoln I. Diuguid, had endured as a chemistry and physical science teacher for more than 30 years at Harris-Stowe Teachers College in St. Louis. I left my telephone number and opened the door to her inviting me into her classroom as a visitor. "Perhaps that is a way to begin moving toward the bigger article that you envision, that led you to write in the first place," I said in closing.

A few days later, we talked by phone and agreed on a date in the fall of 1995 that I would, for the first time, take a seat in Bennett's classroom. What the suburban teacher had called "a tough assignment" was about to start for me: her charge had been for me to "find an instructional way to tell what happened so that kids will learn; parents, administrators and the community will be supportive; and suffering teachers will keep the spark that she lost when she flamed out." I was setting out to experience and tell the stories of public education—from the inside.

Part I
Chapter 2
Getting Involved

Teaching should never be a humdrum, solitary pursuit. Educators and the community must take risks if the outcome is to improve the education of children.

PORTRAIT:
Beatrice McKindra

Beatrice McKindra survived the onslaught of the tornadoes that struck the Kansas City area in May 2003. But the house where she and her husband, Howard, had lived for 30 years and raised their children didn't. Yet, like Alice Bennett, she, too, has shown great tenacity and endurance in the face of difficult circumstances. Her reaction to the storm disaster: "I am extremely thankful to God for allowing us to come through that unscathed. I keep thinking, He must have something for me to do; something is not finished, I guess, or something I need to start is not finished."

As if she hasn't done enough already! For one thing, McKindra has devoted her life to teaching. Originally from Bigelow, Ark., she got her bachelor's degree in 1965 from the College of the Ozarks, now called the University of the Ozarks, in Clarksville, Ark. She began her teaching career right afterward, at about age 21, at Sumner High School in Kansas City, Kan. It was from this school that the black intelligentsia of the town graduated. McKindra recalled that school districts like Kansas City, Kan., were recruiting black students from southern colleges, which is how she and some of her classmates landed in the Midwest.

In 1969 McKindra earned her master's degree from

Emporia State University in Emporia, Kan. But before that she got married in 1968 to Howard McKindra. Their first child, Leilana, was born Sept. 20, 1973, and their twins, Traci and Travis, on Jan. 25, 1980. Leilana was an Alpha Kappa Alpha debutant in 1991, as was her sister, Traci, in 1997. That was the year McKindra let me study with her students at Washington High School. Both of the McKindras' daughters eventually joined that African-American sorority. The couple's three children went on to college and now have successful careers.

McKindra taught in the Kansas City, Kan., School District for 34 years. In the early 1990s she was voted Teacher of the Year. Her retirement coincided with my completion of my studies with the Class of 1999 at Washington High School. Since then she has been substitute teaching in Kansas City, Kan., schools.

McKindra said she had expected to work three more years, but the changes in education that continued to whipsaw teachers around caused her to leave early. The camaraderie among teachers seemed to plummet while low morale reached epidemic levels.

"It was so much lower when I quit than when I started," McKindra said. "We had played together. Maybe it was part of my youth."

Cynicism also infected the teaching profession. Support from the administration was questionable. "If we made a mistake administrators didn't jump on you in parent conferences," McKindra said of her early years. "They kind of stood behind you. Now it's iffy."

She said teaching when she began was really a joy. But when she left, for a lot of educators "it was just a job."

"That I don't like," McKindra added.

There is supposed to be a magic associated with teaching so that educators are excited about what each new day will bring. They're turned on by students' eagerness to learn. Those intoxicating things, which kept teachers like McKindra going, are mostly gone now. She also said she loved the mystery of not knowing how the work she and other teachers did would affect the future for children, their families and the community. "I always hope that I didn't affect them negatively," McKindra said.

Her devotion and concern continue to shine.

*T*he morning was cold November 2, 1995, when I walked from the parking lot overlooking the Washington High School track and football field to the three-story brick building that contained Alice Bennett's classroom. I was dressed in a suit and tie and had on my black overcoat when I grabbed the doorknob and entered Room 43, Bennett's pale green classroom. Bennett introduced me to her 9:15 a.m. third-hour freshman English class, and I took a seat with the students near the chalkboard under a U.S. flag that was bolted to the north wall.

My being at Washington High School and Bennett's allowing me there represented a huge risk for both of us. Before I finally arrived, I asked her to make sure that school district officials were keenly aware that I was in her classes and why I was there. Bennett told me years later that she had subverted the system and had not cleared my presence prior to my arrival in her classroom with anyone in the administration. I also was out on that limb with her. No one at *The Star* knew of our gambit until weeks later. What is clear is no teacher who wants to maintain a career and credibility with parents, students and school district officials could be quoted in a daily newspaper stridently stating what Bennett had shared with me in her letters. She and I both knew that. And no newspaper would allow a journalist to spend costly amounts of time in a school with no clear idea of a return on the investment. Yet what Bennett and I knew was inside Washington High School was a story that had never been told about education, and I wanted to tell it for the benefit of readers with children in inner-city schools.

Over the years my colleagues throughout the country in print and broadcast journalism have told me that starting the Washington High School project was something that they never would have done. The time commitment was too great and the potential for stories was too uncertain. An editor at *The New York Times* said he couldn't believe that I had gotten the newspaper to run the columns, that I was given unfettered access to an inner-city public school, where anything could go wrong, and that I was allowed to quote the students using their names. It was unheard of in journalism.

The project was apparently unheard of in education circles as well. Not even my father, who had been an educator for more than 30 years, offered any support for what I was starting. He said no teacher in her or his right mind would want that interference in the classroom. Several teachers I've interviewed concurred, telling me that they chose the education profession because they loved the independence. Teaching is like being a small business owner, and the success of a teacher's students is an indication that the teacher had enjoyed a good year in turning out a good product. Close scrutiny of how that product was "made" is not always welcomed.

It was no small wonder, then, that Bennett got almost no support or feedback from her co-workers or the parents of her students because she reached out to me. What she had done went against the grain of the way things have always been, and nothing like this had ever been attempted. Anyone who would let me in her classroom has to have a lot of courage; don't underestimate that. How many people would want a journalist watching and taking detailed notes on what they do on the job, how well they communicate with others and scouring every action and everything in their environment for flaws? I had a television crew follow me for three days in the summer of 1998 filming a "Reunion" program on my 25th high school reunion for the Learning Channel, and that was painful. Imagine, however, being the focus of that kind of media scrutiny for an entire school year—which is what Mrs. Bennett was—instead of just three days.

I have called Mrs. Bennett my Harriet Tubman in education. Tubman, a 19th century runaway slave turned Underground Railroad conductor, put her life at risk to lead hundreds of other slaves in the South to freedom in the North. Bennett, like Tubman, put her career at risk to help me in my journey to a free and unfettered look inside the system of public education.

Because the project was so risky, it seemed as if some people were waiting for it to blow up in our faces. It's also why I waited until I had studied with the students over the course of several weeks before I started to write. I needed to reacquaint myself with the day-to-day learning in the classroom, and get to know the students, their hopes and their dreams before I plunged into trying to tell this story to others. I went in absolutely ignorant and with no expectations for what the outcome might be, but I listened and I took a lot of notes.

Something was immediately obvious as I took a seat in Bennett's class: there was hope. In spite of the despair in her letters, she had not given up trying to reach the students, and many of them still had the optimism and eagerness of youth scripted on their faces. She had to perform for those who still wanted to learn and insisted on never abandoning the fact that they, too, had a future. But Bennett also had to put on her best teaching face for this outsider in her class taking notes possibly for all the metropolitan area to read. The situation reminded me of when student teachers from what's now called Harris-Stowe State College in St. Louis would "observe" the classes I was in at Waring Elementary School. The performance of our teachers and the behavior of the students were decidedly different when we had the note-taking college students as guests. It became clear to me that outside involvement could still influence classroom dynamics. Students could discover what the community standards were and teachers could be encouraged to turn out students well-prepared for success in tomorrow's workplace.

But despite the positive influence my presence in the classroom could have, I really hoped to become "invisible." I wanted to be like the inspirational posters that teachers use to decorate their classrooms and that kids from elementary to high school hardly notice. The posters have become so commonplace that the students don't realize they are there. That was my goal at Washington High School. I hoped to go to class so much and on such an unannounced, unpredictable schedule that I would effectively disappear to the students, while remaining very visible for the teachers.

In fact, Bennett and I had many insightful chats after her classes. She helped me make sense of each day, and I served as her sounding board, listening to her concerns and hopes. For example, on November 17, 1995, after a visit at the school, I wrote in my notebook that Bennett and I chatted after the students had gone. She said they had been difficult during a writing session the day before. Ink and paper often bring out the worst in people who are accustomed to making their way through school on bluff and bluster. But on this day of reading and learning they were cooperative and involved.

And I'll never forget December 18, 1995. On that day before the Christmas break, Bennett shook my hand after I had sat through three of her English classes and said she had enjoyed having me in her classroom as if the short time we'd had together was all there was to be. I laughed and said it was only the beginning. I returned at the start of the new semester to my desk in her classroom. My first column on the project ran under the headline **"Becoming part of the class."**

A desk too small in the back of Room 43 welcomed me to a new semester this week at Washington High School.

I've sat there a lot lately. I have ridden that hard student desk for several days in November, December and now January and taken notes in Bennett's freshman English classes.

I took the seat after reading Bennett's plaintive letters in September. I plan to return to the school the rest of the year.

Sure I took freshman English 27 years ago, but corresponding and talking with Bennett showed me that I had new things to learn and that she and her students had a lot to teach.

I wanted to see, hear and feel what it's like to be a teenager today in high school. I also wanted to know firsthand the ups, the downs and the challenges people like Bennett face just doing the job of teaching our kids.

I plan to show and tell what I learn in columns this year. Bennett's letters told of past problems, including guns, drugs, sex and violence in school.

Too many teachers survive by promoting their unteachable and unmanageable problems into someone else's classroom. I wanted to see, so I took my seat in Bennett's classes Nov. 2, 1995.

That day four students slept intermittently, and others wandered in and out of the classroom. The rest took turns reading a book aloud. It was the only way Bennett could ensure that the work would get done. What was lost was time the students should have had for independent study and time the teacher needed to get the students to critically evaluate and analyze the material.

Some read well. Others struggled. Bennett was caught in the middle, trying to keep the good students from glazing over with boredom and slow students from giving up. Disruptions occur when the teacher's grip slips on students at either end. I haven't seen that happen in Bennett's classes so far.

But a couple of unexpected things have occurred. Students initially ignored me until they saw that I kept coming back.

Their faces stuck in my mind, and mine stayed in theirs. One student, Toussaint Turner, and I recognized each other at the 1,000 Man March and Black Expo '95 last month in Kansas City. That was really cool.

In class, students have watched me take notes, asked why and then gotten more interested in school, too. Benoyd Ellison, an assistant principal, came to class on one of my visits and was impressed by the kids' performance.

"This is just beautiful," he said of the quiet, busy students.

"We've had a great day," Bennett said, complimenting the class. "I've really enjoyed you guys today."

I think the kids were just reacting to having a non-disciplining, nonjudgmental adult in the room. It was as if they were just saying, "Pay attention to us. Give us more of your time. That's what we hunger for."

Bennett said the students are also studious when a parent takes a chair in the room. I've just stayed longer.

Bennett has invited me and different classes to pull our desks out of neat rows and into a big circle for discussions about writing, getting good grades and life. I shared stories with the students, and they've spoken volumes to me.

On Thursday we enjoyed reading "Romeo and Juliet."

It's encouraging to note that urban kids still dream of growing up, going to college and becoming somebody. They want to be actors, marine biologists, physicians, singers, lawyers, ballplayers, sportswriters, sports statisticians, Marines, police officers and missionaries.

In the last few weeks I have read the students' work and noted their grades, and some have read their essays to me. It takes courage to read to a stranger, but I guess I'm not much of a stranger to many of them anymore.

In going to Washington High School, I never had an agenda beyond learning as much as possible by seeing what the people at the school saw every day. I never expected to experience anything spectacular. I only wanted to watch the teachers engage the students, witness the learning process, and take the commonplace and reflect it back using the mirror of the press so that it became real to the public and even to the players on the stage of the daily high school dramas. Bennett, for example, made it easy for her students, who might never read *The Kansas City Star*, to suddenly become avid followers of what I had written about her, their school and them. She posted the columns I did by the door on her classroom wall, and the students eagerly watched for them. It made things they normally took for granted seem larger than life and gave me instant feedback on my work. And the longer I stayed, the more evident it became that my "only wanting to watch" was turning into participating, caring, even influencing.

I've been quizzed by people familiar with the canons of journalism about my involvement with the Class of 1999. They've wanted to know whether I got too close and became too wrapped up in the lives of the teachers, students and parents. They'd ask incredulously, "Where is the objective detachment that is supposed to be a hallmark of good journalism?"

Tom Eblen, a former managing editor of *The Kansas City Star* and now retired professor of the William Allen White School of Journalism and Mass Communications at the University of Kansas, helped me with part of the answer to that question. He'd found in following the Washington High School series that a columnist *can* tell such a story well *precisely* because of the point of view, opinion and active involvement that he or she can inject into the assignment and the writing.

When I was in college, one of the best things that I did was to have a double major in news writing and editing and then photojournalism at the University of Missouri-Columbia School of Journalism. In news writing and editing we were told as students to get the story, period. In photojournalism we were instructed to put the camera down when necessary. Don't take that picture if the choice is capturing a person who's suffering or helping the individual in need. All of my career I often have acted more like a photojournalist than as a reporter or editor. I have done the profane and the unmentionable when it comes to turning my back on what Joe or Josephine Journalism would insist that I do when people have needed someone to coddle them.

I found myself many times in Bennett's classes putting my pen down to help the students know that I cared. Each time I went to that classroom—and I went at least once a week and stayed for three to five classes—I'd leave there deeply moved by what I'd experienced.

As mere observers, people come to things with their own lens. Adults often approach young people from a belittling and condescending perspective, rather than seeing them as they see themselves. Yet teens have the ability to educate us; we just have to be open-minded enough to be taught.

Students also have only one shot at an education, and it's important that they have some sense that they're being heard and what they're going through is being taken seriously by everyone. Dispassionate yet hypercritical adults have dominated too many things in their lives. They need someone who will listen and accurately communicate their concerns without being judgmental. That's why it's important as a journalist to put down the pen and notepad, to push aside the reporter's objectivity, and to get involved.

Many of the columns that I wrote on the project exposed the times that I couldn't help but get involved with the students. Toward the end of my second year at the school, I wrote a column headlined, **"Time hasn't muffled the message."** Bennett had gotten me a seat with many of the same students and many new ones in Beatrice McKindra's English classes.

Beatrice McKindra's kids at Washington High School wanted me to read to them even though a cold had the best of me.

But learning is a participatory sport. The sophomores in McKindra's 7:30 a.m. English class knew that I was always eager to play the game, especially when the book was Harper Lee's *To Kill a Mockingbird*.

The award-winning novel, a piece of modern Americana, is the latest thing I've studied with McKindra's kids at Washington High School.

I'd read *To Kill a Mockingbird* more than 27 years ago when I was in high school. But the story came alive again when I read a few pages aloud to the first-hour class. It was as if I'd never put the book down. The discussions that McKindra has led have been wonderful.

Prejudice, justice and human dignity are recurring themes in the book, McKindra has told her first- and second-hour classes. Many of the students identified with Scout, the tomboy, the no-nonsense central character who tells the story in retrospect.

"I like Scout," said Steve Brown, one of McKindra's second-hour kids. "She ain't no punk."

The class laughed. McKindra responded, "She isn't a punk."

51

The students could also relate to Scout's older brother, Jem, and other characters, even though the story was set in the South decades before they were born. Jem, Scout and their friends had to use their imagination, curiosity and ingenuity to fill a lot of playtime in their Maycomb County, Ala., community.

"They didn't have television so they had to create their own games," McKindra said. That included making up stories about Boo Radley. Radley left treasures for the kids in the knothole of a tree and eventually saved Scout's and Jem's lives.

The book told how Scout and Jem had an older dad, Atticus, who was a lawyer, and a black housekeeper, Calpurnia. They taught the children to read at home, which put them ahead of their classmates in school.

McKindra helped the students put that in perspective. It was akin to the students knowing the alphabet and numbers before they got to kindergarten.

The book also contained the tough issue of racism and the town folk calling Scout's family "nigger lovers" because Atticus defended Tom Robinson, a black man accused of raping a white woman.

"We're not used to those words, Mrs. McKindra," Markesha Clark said in the first-hour class.

"I don't like to be called that word," she said. "I'm not one of those people.

"It means dumb and stupid, and it's not me."

But the book makes the students walk in those moccasins and overcome the ugliness by giving them a new strength of character. The one thing that doesn't abide by majority rule is a person's conscience, Atticus tells his and McKindra's kids.

McKindra asked her students to name a symbol in the book.

Michelle Hyde said one is the mockingbird.

"It's a sin to kill a mockingbird," Michelle said. "They just sing.

"They do no harm. They just bring happiness."

The students said the book had several mockingbirds, including Boo Radley, Tom Robinson and the children. In them bloom the perennials of innocence, courage, compassion, empathy, pride, respect, curiosity, honesty and justice.

That's a lot. But I'm glad I got to learn it again in a different era and with a new generation at Washington High School.

An interesting note is that a reader in outstate Missouri sent this column to Harper Lee, who lives in Alabama. She wrote him a thank you note, which he then forwarded to me. I shared that note with McKindra and her students and have since corresponded with Harper Lee, mailing to her at her request every one of the columns I have written about Washington High School.

During the time I was with the students I often brought things to class to enhance the learning experience. It dawned on me later, after reviewing Bennett's initiating letters, that my bringing extra things to class was part of her intent long before I angered her with the column on the suburban teacher's burnout. Bennett's original letter contained references to a column headlined **"Education helps purge untrue images, intimidate status quo,"** that I had written a full year before I started attending her classes. In that column I described how I walked the streets of Kansas City dressed in a T-shirt that said "Danger: Educated Blackman." My wife thought the shirt, which I had bought at a National Association of Black Journalists convention in Detroit, was too incendiary. But Bennett thought it might spur the black students in her classes to learn. Her insight as a white teacher with a black husband and son helped her realize the value in getting minority students to realize their potential through education, as educated people of color.

Percy Penn and I rode the escalator at downtown City Center Square. On the ride up I asked him what he thought about my shirt. The urban planner and former Kansas State University professor put his hand on my shoulder and smiled.

He looked at the extra-large black T-shirt flaming with red, black and white lettering that said, "DANGER: EDUCATED BLACKMAN."

"Blackman" was one word, like superman. The full-chest emblem resembled signs that warn people of life-threatening situations.

I bought the T-shirt at a black arts festival and picked up a matching "Blackwoman" shirt for my wife. Then I modeled my T-shirt on Main Street recently to see how people would react.

A lot of folks did neck-twisting double takes. Most smiled. A few frowned. But the shirt got people to think and talk about race relations—a danger zone we too often detour around. The T-shirt, with its dark humor, also hit on the unease educated black people sometimes feel because stereotypes and stigmas surrounding quotas paint us as less qualified than whites.

Because educated people of color don't fit that image, we're sometimes viewed as a threat. A danger we face is the added stress and hypertension of trying to be supermen and superwomen in dispelling falsehoods.

On my walk downtown I collected thoughts from white and black people. Penn, who is black, said educated African-American men could contribute more to our democracy if others' low expectations didn't bar their way.

Donald L. Anderson, an Internal Revenue Service agent who is black, said, "You can sense that there is a certain fear of us—maybe not a fear of us but a desire not to deal with us in the same manner that they deal with others."

Anderson also shared the views of black teenage sisters

54

Valerie and Veronica Smith.

"It seems like there are so few of us," Anderson said. "It's more like endangered than danger."

But Frank Williams, who is white and Anderson's co-worker, offered another thought: "The more people know, the more reasonable they can be about things. I don't think ignorance is bliss. I think education is."

The T-shirt caught Milinda Seemann's eye outside City Center Square. It's a statement about respect, said Seemann, who is white and works in banking.

Dorothy Mozee, a black woman who works at the nearby Hereford House restaurant, said the T-shirt reminded her of her grandson at Central Missouri State University. Educated black men are competition and a threat to the status quo.

"A lot of black men aren't considered as educated," said John Townsend, a black man and financial adviser with Associates Financing. Too many are thought to have no future.

That's why a good education and impressing our children of its importance are critical, Townsend said at the Town Pavilion.

I left Main Street and drove to the Lucile Bluford Branch Library in the black community, where posters of Malcolm X and the Rev. Martin Luther King Jr. said, "Great Minds Meet at the Library." People inside were too busy to talk.

This is one of our city's mental weight rooms, where people go to build strong minds. Another poster said, "A Human Mind Once Stretched Never Returns To Its Former Dimensions."

I then drove to the University of Missouri-Kansas City and walked through the campus. Colleges are construction zones for revolutionary thought.

Pre-med student Michael Bobo, who is black, shouted, "Great shirt!" He said he only wished more black people would enroll to get high on learning.

I agree. There's no danger—just a great future—in that.

Those T-shirts, which are now the property of the Black Archives of Mid-America Inc. in Kansas City, proclaimed the importance and power of being an educated person of color. In order to reach that goal, however, students must be exposed to the achievements of their own ethnic group—as well as to those of others'. Bennett allowed me to give a few gifts of multicultural education to her students at Washington High School, and I wrote about one of those opportunities in a column headlined **"Inspiring a new generation."**

Alice Bennett and her ninth-grade English classes helped me find new meaning in old poetry.

In honor of Black History Month, I had the students read inspirational African-American literature containing strong messages of an oppressed people overcoming enormous odds.

Students need the power of such enduring prose to carry them past drugs, alcohol, gangs, violence, crime, teen pregnancy, AIDS and suicide. The black voices have given faith and hope to generations of people since the Harlem Renaissance after World War I. They can guide today's youth, too.

One poem was Claude McKay's classic, "If We Must Die." The Jamaican-born author studied at what then was called Kansas State College. He wrote "If We Must Die" in 1919 in response to what the Encyclopedia of Black America called an "unparalleled eruption of racial violence." Black people were migrating from farm-fed destitution in the South to jobs in the North.

The shift worsened the tension in cities between blacks and whites competing for jobs, housing and other necessities. Black blood flowed through shootings, lynchings, burnings and assaults in what became known as "the Red Summer of 1919."

Jarome Willingham, 16; Terry Wheat, 15; Greg Lee, 16; and Corey Brinton, 15, read McKay's poem aloud in Bennett's four classes:

If we must die, let it not be like hogs,
Hunted and penned in an inglorious spot,
While round us bark the mad and hungry dogs,
Making their mock at our accursed lot.
If we must die, O let us nobly die,
So that our precious blood may not be shed
In vain; then even the monsters we defy
Shall be constrained to honor us though dead!
O Kinsmen! we must meet the common foe!
Though far outnumbered, let us show us brave,
And for their thousand blows, deal one deathblow!
What though before us lies the open grave?
Like men we'll face the murderous, cowardly pack,
Pressed to the wall, dying, but fighting back!

Corey said it was a poem about gaining respect. Greg and Jarome said it spoke of strength. Terry said it symbolized black resistance since slavery.

I told the students that I had learned in college that British Prime Minister Winston Churchill had McKay's poem posted in his fighter pilots' cockpits during World War II.

Then Bennett added that she thought the poem spoke to 1990s problems of drive-by shootings, youth violence and senseless urban slaughter.

Examples are the slayings of Frank Fontana, 31, killed in a drive-by shooting at the Edge, 323 W. Eighth St. in Kansas City, Mo.; and Tiffany Davis, 16, gunned down at a party in the 1700 block of Quindaro Boulevard in Kansas City, Kan.

"There's nothing noble about a young person dying in a senseless drive-by shooting," Bennett said. The shooters "are cowards hiding in cars."

I told the students to arm themselves with education to fight violence. Studying the past will get them through the problems of the present.

"I think writing like this stands the test of time," Bennett said. "It talks to today's youth. The current runs true."

It runs deep, too.

My inability to avoid involvement in the classes was part of the benefit I derived from the dare that started it all. I saw that students don't learn in a vacuum, and teachers don't teach in one. Everything around school encroaches on their experiences and influences the outcome. It is, therefore, vital that schools not be seen as isolation units, but that teachers reach out as the community reaches in.

The public has to support teachers and our system of public education or our community risks losing the good teachers, the schools as the centerpieces of society and eventually the way of life that allows people to live in peace and prosper. People must value the vast experience that teachers have in educating our children. They must visit schools and teachers and remain active and involved in classroom work. Parents and other adult visitors then serve as teachers' allies. All help raise the level of academic performance for teachers and students, who remain at their best when visitors are in the room.

The challenges facing today's students, teachers and schools can seem overwhelming, even insurmountable. Yet my experience showed me that they are not impossible to overcome. Students and teachers face them with courage and optimism—and with the help of outside involvement. For four years after the May 31, 1995, column that started the chain of two teachers' reactions, I would go back to school to listen, to try to discover just what kind of world urban high school students and teachers face today, and to describe it to the community, perhaps hoping that others, too, will listen and get involved.

Part II
Chapter 3
Preconceived Notions Challenged

Being in the schools and so very close to the students and teachers causes widely held myths about education to dissolve. The truth makes accepting the falsehoods about public schools impossible.

PORTRAIT:
Scott Milkowart

I sat in Scott Milkowart's class when the students were juniors. He was much younger than McKindra and Bennett. He still had the magic dust of enthusiasm from college sprinkled all over him. The relationship I had with him was different from the rapport I had with Bennett and McKindra. In our before- and after-school conversations, he'd sometimes turn the tables so that I became the teacher and he was the interested student. We talked about investments, homeownership, cars, his students, my spouse and his girlfriend, possible career moves and sports. I got to know and correspond with his parents in Kansas and grandmother in a small town in New York. As a favor to Milkowart, I mailed them the columns I did about his class at Washington High School. He is a dedicated teacher who has a lot to offer. That came out in a column I did headlined, **"Why teach in the city? Why not?"** I learned a lot about incentives that have been in place to get people like Milkowart to start their careers in urban areas.

Scott Milkowart's troops wouldn't come out of their trenches at Washington High School.

He had a lot of ground to cover on World War I in his American history class. He also had the video "All Quiet on the Western Front" to show students the horrors of war.

But his interactive efforts last week fell on an unresponsive room. It was an eerie lesson.

Milkowart was exasperated. No one responded when he asked the names of countries on Germany's western and eastern borders where most of the fighting occurred. He asked the students what happened to Russia in 1917 and how that affected World War I.

"We spent over a week on this stuff," he said.

I tried to give Milkowart a pep talk after his video rescue. I blamed the rain and spring fever for the students' apathy. I can see the war's fingers reaching into today's global conflicts. But it didn't excite the students.

Maybe Alice Bennett was right.

Urban teachers often hit these walls of blank stares and dumbfounding silence.

But despite the silence and other challenges, Milkowart, 31, said teaching in an urban district was his choice. He could be the poster dude for a government loan program encouraging people to teach in urban districts.

The football and track coach grew up in Herington, Kan., and graduated from the University of Kansas (KU). He put himself through school on loans, scholarships and jobs. About $7,200 of that came from a Perkins loan.

The beauty of the Perkins loan is it can be canceled if an education graduate works in an urban district.

"The idea behind that is to encourage people to give back to the community," said Lisa Santa Maria, director of the Perkins Loan Program at KU. She said 900 Perkins loans had been issued this fiscal year at the 27,500-student university.

The money goes to students who become teachers in special-needs areas, nurses, medical technicians, child or family services workers for high-risk low-income children, military personnel in hostile places, full-time law enforcement officers, Head Start workers, or Peace Corps or VISTA volunteers.

"It's the oldest student-aid program out there," Santa Maria said. It began in 1950 and was named after the late Rep. Carl D. Perkins.

Milkowart had done his student teaching in the Blue Valley district. But he wanted a more culturally diverse classroom experience for his career. He was hired at Washington High School in August 1995. It was a good choice.

"I think I've become a better teacher because of it," Milkowart said. "There are situations in my school that just don't happen in other schools."

He and his colleagues help students learn and cope with myriad school, home and urban upheavals.

"They are more magnified than in other places," Milkowart said. "They're more visible."

But, he added, maybe the money in the suburbs just covers up the problems.

I think he's right.

*I*n December 1995, I was in a discussion about good journalism. A dialogue started on public education issues. People shared thoughts that included the worst stories about inner city schools. They lamented poor attendance, high crime, absence of parent involvement, mismanagement and high dropout rates. Normally I would have agreed with what was said and would have furthered the discussion. But the conversation I heard suddenly seemed shortsighted, misdirected, cliché and trite. I had been sitting in Alice Bennett's freshman English classes before Christmas break, taking notes and gathering information for the launch the following January of what became a four-year series of columns on Washington High School. That experience had changed me and my understanding of the people and issues entangled in the daily struggle to get our children to learn. I tried to inject the new reality I had experienced into the dialogue. But the stereotypes about inner-city schools were too strong; what I said then went against everything others had read and experienced as journalists who mostly skirt the periphery of education.

I encountered similar reactions based on stereotypes during a question and answer session after a Feb. 9, 1999, speech I gave in south Kansas City on Solutions for Our Community's Redemption. A gentleman in the audience asked a revealing question. He had followed the series of columns on Washington High School and challenged me to explain why they left him with the impression that life in public schools was mostly positive. I had led him to believe that the students were mostly good kids and that teachers were still able to get young people to learn. I told him that's because the reality of being in the schools is vastly different from what people pick up in the media, which tell us that education and public schools are troubled places where kids are homicidal and no learning takes place.

Even teachers hold similar strong biases, as I found out during a continuing education class for teachers. The course instructors tried to get across to about 150 educators that gangs and drugs are as much a part of life in wealthy suburbs such as Johnson County, Kan., as they are in the inner-city of Kansas City, Mo., and Kansas City, Kan. I wrote about the lessons that came from the class in a column headlined **"Wake up and read the graffiti"** (see Appendix). But what fascinated me just as much were the questions the teachers from throughout the area asked Kansas City police Officer Jennifer Wolf. Questions often reveal a person's mindset and intent. None of the ones that teachers asked Wolf tracked with her earlier discussion on her career and gang awareness. Instead, the teachers wanted to know about Wolf's gun and whether she had fired it, and each answer she gave yielded more off-beat questions that revealed prejudices against youths. It was as if the teachers had suddenly gotten to quiz a star of a police drama series, and they were making the most of the opportunity. They wanted to know about the "bad guys," whether police treated "those people" sternly enough and whether the rights of the accused superseded the rights of the victims. But the questions were coded so that the "bad guys" were always wrong and often black, whereas the police were always right. To the audience, racial profiling was acceptable in most circumstances, and how dare victims' rights take a back seat to constitutional protections for people accused of crimes. These teachers were "A" students of media stereotypes, and it blatantly showed.

It made me wonder how they kept those biases from oozing into the lectures they give students in classrooms and whether they realized the seepage was taking place or if they tried to prevent it from happening. In fact, I had seen first-hand what was arguably an example of teacher bias and recorded it in a column headlined, **"Heritage, pride enrich education."** During a visit to a local elementary school I had

helped tutor a student struggling with math. The African-American boy beamed when he realized that, with a little coaching, he could figure out the division problems, too.

I stepped back to allow him to work on his own. That's when the teacher deflated the moment, telling me: "He'll never learn. He's so lazy."

SuEllen Fried, who co-authored *Bullies, Targets & Witnesses: Helping Children Break the Pain Chain* with her daughter, Paula Fried, said something profound that fits situations like this, which unfortunately are repeated hundreds of thousands of times behind closed doors in schools nationwide. Fried said in an interview that a principal in Fort Myers, Fla., told her after one of her workshops on bullying: "There is a saying among principals —'Feed the teachers so they don't eat the students.'" That chewing up and chewing out of the students often are expressed in biases teachers might harbor that seem to surface innocently or subconsciously. Yet the damage that is done to the children in negative self-fulfilling prophesies and in lowering the expectations of what students might achieve often is irreparable. It's why teachers should never be bullied, and parents and other adults in the community must develop a strong rapport with educators akin to what happens in journalism when good reporters have exceptional professional relationships with their best sources. Together educators working with and for the community can achieve the best outcomes for all students.

In a graduation speech that I later gave at Chick Elementary School in Kansas City, Mo., an African-centered school where Black heritage is woven into the curriculum (and in the **"Heritage, pride enrich education"** column) I wondered

> how many children like [the boy in the Kansas City, Kan., elementary school] were being damaged by teachers whose biases lead to self-fulfilling prophecies.
>
> Michelle Campbell, president of M.D. Campbell & Associates, which advises schools on how to better serve the growing diversity in area districts, said it set up what's called the "fourth-grade failure syndrome" for black boys. Many schools, starting in kindergarten, strip those boys of the fun and excitement of learning. Many give up by fourth grade.

Such treatment sets up stunning problems. In an article entitled "A Ghetto Within a Ghetto," Joel McNally puts this tendency in stark statistical terms. He states that "African American children constitute 17 percent of total student enrollment and 33 percent of those now labeled mentally retarded or cognitively disabled." He goes on to add that "[n]ationwide, Blacks are nearly three times more likely to be identified as mentally retarded than white students and nearly twice as likely to be labeled as emotionally disturbed." When it comes to being identified as having "specific

64

learning disabilities," McNally says, "Blacks [are] about 30 percent more likely than whites to be so categorized." Furthermore, "that over-representation in most school districts [seems] to be exclusively among African-American boys."

George C. Fraser, author of *Success Runs in Our Race*, put that same message a little differently in a speech he gave to the National Association of Market Developers, Kansas City chapter. In a column headlined, **"The old challenge is with us still: Triumph over mediocrity,"** I summarized his thoughts:

> Black parents must push their kids to be superachievers because in America their children's talents often will be doubted and discounted based only on the color of their skin.

> "If you are black and mediocre in America, leave," Fraser said. "Because you will continue to be marginalized, and ultimately you will be destroyed."

This marginalization, says McNally, happens not for the reasons that are generally trotted out to rationalize the trend—the consequences of "extreme poverty," including "inadequate pre-natal care, poor nutrition, drug and alcohol consumption during pregnancy, or childhood environmental hazards." Rather it happens, according to Gary Orfield, co-director of Harvard University's Civil Rights Project, because "white teachers . . . don't understand how to deal with young Black boys who are acting out . . . and there are no social services available in schools" to help them work with "kids who have problems they can't deal with" (qtd. in McNally).

At Washington High School, I learned that the socialization and education of young people occurs in the margins of everything else. In communities of color in America's urban cores, people live stretched lives, taut with agony over jobs, crime, urban decay, truncated life expectancy, poor housing and other American Dream deficiencies. Imagine how that flows into America's schools. Look at students' young lives as a paper given a teacher for her review. Teachers normally require papers from students to have standard margins. That gives educators space to write in praise, corrections and guidance, all of which helps young people to improve. But young urban students bring to school issues that overflow the pages of their lives. Not only are the margins in some troubled communities perilously narrow, but often there are no margins at all. Just getting by for many African-American, Latino, Native American and other poor kids fills up and often spills off the pages of what teachers daily see in their interaction with students. It not only makes the students' lives appear incomprehensible to educators, who are mostly white and grew up in middle-class suburban environments, but it also leaves the teachers no room and no space to write in the margins of the kids' lives. It excludes many opportunities for instructors to offer guidance, corrections, support, and praise which are always needed in the education process of every child. This is especially detrimental to children whose lives are "marginalized" and who are starving for understanding and constructive interaction with, even encouragement from caring adults. This analogy helps me, as a journalist, visualize why there are communication gulfs between students, teachers and parents.

In journalism, communication is a currency—as it is in education. Communication currency exchanges must take place for learning to occur. If teachers can't decipher the script overflowing the pages of students' lives, they can't communicate effectively with those young people. The currency of education undergoes a relentless devaluation as students progress through primary and secondary education. This sets them up to be constantly and deeply misunderstood.

These trends and the resulting stereotyping are at least in part due to two major forces in today's society. The first is the changing demographics of our communities and the insufficient training teachers have to help them adjust their focus and teaching methods to those changes. The second, which I mentioned at the beginning of this chapter and will elaborate on below, is the media misrepresentation of schools and society.

Changing Demographics

Gary R. Howard brings the new reality about our changing demographics into focus. Many educators desperately need to read his book, *We Can't Teach What We Don't Know: White Teachers, Multiracial Schools.* Howard notes, for example, that students of color reached 30 percent of the total number of kids in our schools in 1990. That number grew to 34 percent in 1994 and will jump to 40 percent by 2010 (2). Here's the disconnect. In 1993 whites constituted 90 percent of public school teachers, a figure that could grow in the coming years (2). Howard added that

the need for teacher preparation [in multicultural education and better communication skills with minorities] is obvious, particularly given the fact most practicing and prospective White teachers are themselves the products of predominantly White neighborhoods and predominantly White colleges of teacher education . . . . Over 86 percent of White suburbanites live in neighborhoods that are less than 1 percent Black . . . , and it is precisely these kinds of middle-class White communities that will continue to provide the bulk of our public school teachers. (2)

This lack of exposure makes it difficult for them to understand the differences posed by minority students. The disconnect surfaces when many of these teachers insist on treating all children the same whereas they are all different and should be treated as such. In other words, the disconnect comes from applying the Golden Rule rather than what diversity experts refer to as the Platinum Rule. The Golden Rule admonishes us to treat other people as we ourselves would prefer to be treated. That would mean, for instance, that I should treat women as I would want to be treated when we all know that men and women are very different. And students come in many more varieties—not just male and female. Black, white, Hispanic, Asian American and Native American students are all different, which is why educators would be more effective if they followed the Platinum Rule, which tells us to *treat others as they themselves would prefer to be treated.* If teachers don't realize this, however, communication can break down. Stereotypes take over. Students stop learning and could start living *down* to the teachers' biases. A self-fulfilling prophecy emerges. Therefore, educators have to get to know the students, the parents and the people in the community, and know how to communicate effectively with them so that learning can take place in the classroom.

One way to achieve this is for teachers to actually live in the attendance area of the schools where they work. I learned this from talking with a group of octogenarians who graduated together from an inner-city elementary school in 1930 and have remained bonded as friends who regularly get together. They explained to me what teaching was like when they were kids and the sense of community they enjoyed. For example, 70 years ago, school-teachers could call on parents to take them to the store, downtown or to fetch them anything they needed. That was what people did then for teachers. No request was too great. The teachers lived in the attendance area of the school, and everyone felt honored—and even competed—to serve the educators and the administrators.

A way to diminish the classroom disconnect between inner-city kids and their suburban teachers is to re-establish that sense of commitment and community. I think teachers care more about the kids and the community if their homes and other property are in that community, and if their paychecks aren't exported to another area, but are spent at vital local businesses. They then have a personal, vested interest in being more concerned and in caring about what goes on with the students in and around their school. Parents, in turn, would be better able to renew that feeling of serving teachers if those same teachers were their neighbors who demonstrated their commitment to the community surrounding the school. All would benefit from the exposure to each other as they shared the burden of educating the multicultural young people of the community.

In addition, for Howard, preparing teachers for a multicultural classroom environment goes hand-in-hand with acknowledging white privilege. He cites the groundbreaking work on white privilege done by Peggy McIntosh, Associate Director of the Center for

Research on Women at Wellesley College in Massachusetts, and writes that "[s]ocial positionality for Whites in Western societies has afforded us a personal sense of invisibility related to the unfolding drama of dominance . . . . And without acknowledging the reality of dominance, we could not engage in a discussion of strategies for change" (30). He adds: "That our privileged dominance often threatens the physical and cultural well-being of other groups is a reality that Whites, for the most part, have chosen to ignore. The fact that we *can* choose to ignore such realities is perhaps our most insidious privilege" (62).

From his perspective as a white educator, he acknowledges that "[f]or white educators it is especially important that we lift the curtain of ignorance and denial that has protected us from understanding our location on the broader stage of hierarchical social arrangements. We need to see how the lives of our students have been scripted by their membership in groups differing in degrees of social dominance and marginality" (31).

By finally recognizing and acknowledging the diversity of the student population because of the changing demographics, teachers can adapt their teaching style—so that no student is stereotyped, erroneously labeled as "cognitively disabled," or simply brushed off as "so lazy . . . he'll never learn." No child, truly, should be left behind. It has to be more than a catchy political slogan.

Media misrepresentation

The media have not helped in dispelling prevalent stereotypes and myths. Many of the shows that are young people's favorites today are feeding them harmful stereotypes about African-Americans. For example, police dramas often show crime occurring mostly in black neighborhoods. But as Farai Chideya points out in her book *Don't Believe the Hype: Fighting Cultural Misinformation about African Americans,* "It may be the media's best kept secret: The majority of violent criminals are white" (198).

Then there are talk shows, which dress up folks with the oddest problems and parade them before cameras as if that's middle America. In addition, music videos and many other shows aimed at young people make women out to be sex toys for men.

None of that is everyday reality. Unbleached wholesomeness is missing in the media. Chideya writes: "The entire hard-working, typical center of the black community drops out of media coverage" (4). Through the media's eyes, whites see black people as "unproductive and often dangerous members of this society" (4). Media stereotypes support the "pathology" that stains African-Americans as "the worst America has to offer" (5), Chideya adds.

I wrote about the pervasive negative images that are being fed TV-viewers in a column titled, **"Masked in stereotypes, television loses sight of self-esteem"**:

> Horseplay killed our old TV and opened our eyes to the language of television.

> My daughters, Adrianne, 12, and Leslie, 9, smashed into our 1983 set and flat-lined its 25-inch images. I bought a new TV, and it came with closed-captioning, enabling hearing-impaired people to read the rapid-fire dialogue.

> It's wild to watch the type roll onto the screen as fast as people talk. Music symbols tell when a character is humming or singing.

> But I also noticed some disturbing dialogue on some shows. I knew the programs were bad, but seeing the garbage in print exposes the vile media stereotypes of popular shows such as "Martin," "Living Single," "Family Matters," "Fresh Prince of Bel-Air" and "Hangin' with Mr. Cooper."

> Black men are shown as skirt-chasing, shucking-and-jiving, Stepin Fetchit buffoons. Black women are either the straight characters who try to keep their male counterparts in line or they are difficult, ultramaterialistic people with eye-cutting superattitudes. The images appear on screen with broken English, bad grammar and profanity.

70

What's funny is to listen and read at the same time because sometimes the translators clean up the dialogue so much that the words don't match what the characters are saying—just like in dubbed foreign films.

I even shot four rolls of film of the closed-captioned black TV shows to freeze the media stereotypes in pictures, which I showed to University of Kansas journalism students. The prints opened their eyes.

Some examples include: *Cute little gloves, tight little outfit* and *I'm, uh, ain't gonna do nothing,* from "Fresh Prince." From "Living Single": *Overton's with that thin-ankled heifer right now* and *You can't change your mind about no garbage, man.*

From "Martin": *I can bust you up, so you're not worth it* and *Where you at? Where you at, boy?*

New shows like "Moesha" are using the same awful stereotypes.

Such negative stereotypes scar the self-images of black children and families. Attacking the problem is essential.

"We should be heroic in our efforts to promote positive images," said Susan Wilson, a behavioral psychologist in Kansas City. The public needs to be re-educated on what being black in America really is because media stereotypes have negatively altered the truth.

Television shows on African-Americans wouldn't be so bad if they covered the full spectrum of black people in America the same as the media do for whites. That would include serious dramas, programs about working professionals, blue-collar shows, mysteries (and that doesn't include "Cops" or "America's Most Wanted") as well as comedies.

But all black people get are loud laugh tracks on minstrel shows with "Amos and Andy" offsprings. Mixing African-American characters with solid images into mostly white shows isn't good enough when all black shows are so bent toward biases.

The public needs to expect more from television programming than it is getting. Because what we're receiving now from the invasive and powerful image-maker are lies. Our kids see it, mimic it and then own the negative portrayals of themselves. Whites see it and think it's gospel.

This psychological media violence is beating up and flat-lining the good self-images that black kids and adults need in order to survive.

When the media cover society, then, stereotypes and myths are put on display and presented as truth, so that kids are seduced into emulating the behavior and images. That affects urban kids at schools like Washington High. When the media cover education, we normally include stories on the school boards, the elections, administration turmoil, student problems, and education innovations. That is what journalism schools teach and reporters perfect in their careers at newspapers, magazines and in the broadcast media. It is easy and the outcomes are certain. Yet what's always been done in the tradition of covering schools is not good enough, because at the same time this media coverage often emphasizes the negative occurrences at schools— especially inner-city schools— and those stories have made people afraid to go into our schools.

That fear is not entirely unfounded or irrational. The first day I tried to enter Alice Bennett's classroom, the door was locked. Such security measures are part of the landscape of urban public schools. In fact, this project was taking place in the awful urban swirl of gang proliferation and in the fading heyday of crack cocaine. Those twin community thugs walked the streets of the poor and mostly black and Latino neighborhoods of Kansas City, Kan. They added to the misery of crime, white flight to "safe" suburbs and the loss of businesses, jobs, shopping centers, opportunity and hope. Prisons and jails overflowed with young men who got "caught up." So did the hospitals treating the wounds of gangs, gunshot victims and innocent people caught in the crossfire. The churches and cemeteries had to devote an inordinate amount of time and resources to tending to the misery and burying the dead. Families with children, many headed by single parents, were scratching to get by. Because of crack and other drugs, grandparents, aunts and other family members were left to raise children.

This was part of America's Bosnia, Kosovo and Chechnya, where white and middle-class flight allowed an insane kind of ethnic cleansing to occur. The public decries the horrors that people in those countries have had to endure. We open up our hearts to the survivors of mass shootings and killings like the tragedy at Columbine High School near Littleton, Colorado, on April 20, 1999. But we don't shed a tear for the children in places like Kansas City, Kan. The population of the poorest county in the metropolitan area was traumatized as factories closed and people were laid off. Instead of supporting each other, instead of supporting the schools, the overwhelming community stress often caused people to turn on each other with more gun violence, rape, burglaries and robberies. A hidden human suffering occurred daily.

In 1995, Kansas City, Kan., had a record 70 homicides, up from a previous high of 59 set in 1992. The numbers fade in the public's collective memory. The lasting evidence, however, is in the weed-infested vacant lots, boarded-up, rundown buildings, gap-toothed neighborhoods and good land that was never developed. Community stability and prosperity flee such killing fields. In the aftermath, the community looks for all the world as if heated corner-to-corner gunbattles had been waged along the old and disintegrating sidewalks, and bombs had rained on the homes, apartment buildings and businesses. What was clear was that, in this war in American cities like Kansas City, Kan., the people were the victims and the children with all of the mental, emotional and psychological scars of that war were dragging the carnage into the schools, putting all children, teachers and learning at risk.

Yet, in spite of this sad and terrifying backdrop, what I experienced at Washington High School helped me get past the biases and the usual reporting of the negative things that happen in urban schools. I got to see and show the full picture of what takes place in public education. I found that the unseemly things do in fact happen. But they occur in the rivers of everything else. The ugly

73

stuff, however, is what stands out while teachers' day-to-day victories in getting kids to learn flow like water under a bridge—mostly uncaptured and unreported. We in the media feed on the negative. It's the meat and potatoes, the comfort food, in the heavy news diet that we deliver every day to the public. We unnecessarily scare people about kids and about ever thinking of going into inner-city schools.

My studies at Washington High School focused on all aspects of education and found that the young people, educators, schools, learning and events involved in public education—just as in most other aspects of life—are mostly good. I discovered that there was a positive core often obscured by storm clouds of negative public impressions and press about urban schools.

But I also found that the media have created positive myths about other forms of education. One involves homeschooling, which the politics of our times promotes as an alternative to urban schools. We've made it seem so warm, quaint and appealing. But we never show the other side: the culture shock it creates for children and families who rejoin their peers in public schools after being homeschooled. Alice Bennett urged me to examine that aspect through the experiences of a student I got to know in her freshman English class. I did that in a column headlined, **"There's a lot to learn when schools replace home education."**

Adrian Hutson got my attention in Alice Bennett's class.

At times he possesses an enthusiasm that his peers don't. Bennett said that he, like me, is learning what it's like to be a teenager today.

Adrian, 16, went from being homeschooled for six years to public school when he moved from Houston to Kansas City, Kan. On my visits to Bennett's class, I've talked to Adrian and watched him adjust. I'd never encountered a homeschooler when I was in ninth grade 27 years ago. It has helped me learn more about the dynamic mix of people and situations in public education today.

Adrian explained that he'd finished third grade in regular school and then started home school with his brother and sister. He told me how he got his books and course work, adhered to a study regime and was tested on the material.

His mom was his primary teacher. "But we taught ourselves part of the time," Adrian said.

"It was easy at first, and I was kind of excited about it," he said. "Then it got tedious.

"I wouldn't want to do homeschooling again."

Adrian outlined several pitfalls. Siblings normally squabble, but Adrian said that in homeschooling arguments turn into donnybrooks. Adrian said he and his older sister and younger brother stayed at each other's throats.

Adrian said homeschooling also separated him from his peers. "I hardly got out," he said.

"Once you get out you don't know the slang and stuff like that," he said. "People say, 'Boy, is he out of date!'

"You lose contact with the world. Stuff has been going on the past six years, and it's like duh."

Also, most teens just want to fit in with their peers. Adrian said homeschooling in that way was a major liability for him.

"A lot of kids don't want to hang out with me," Adrian said. He blames the isolation of homeschooling, which made him a new kid at Washington High School whether he'd just moved from Houston or not.

"I was with adults," said Adrian, who's thinking about entering the Air Force after high school. "You don't get to be a kid."

Many homeschoolers going to regular school must adjust, said Jennie Ethell, Home School Legal Defense Association media relations liaison. But the rest of the class

75

should make accommodations for the new student, too.

Adrian has managed to pick up some friends, and each day he learns as much about being a teen from his peers as he gets in his education from teachers.

I asked Adrian which was tougher, home school or public school. Adrian weighed the two. High school, he said, is harder.

"It seems like everybody is mean to me—'A new kid: Let's pick on him.' But I don't back down. I never back down."

Yet in home school, sibling conflict was constant, too. The difference was that his home-school adversaries were familiar.

A classmate, De'Angello Hillmon, chimed into the discussion I was having with Adrian. De'Angello thought high school would be harder than homeschooling because at Washington High School people were always making demands.

Adrian tied three rubber bands together as sort of a busy-work distraction and then said the classwork—especially algebra—was harder in high school than in home school.

But he added with the voice of experience about peers who make demands: "In high school you can ignore them. In home school you get in trouble if you ignore things.

"Here, who cares?"

De'Angello reasoned that Adrian cared. He stood up for what he thought was right, he argued and he got angry.

De'Angello's input was positive peer pressure and another lesson for both Adrian and me on being a teen in an urban district today.

I received a lot of feedback from parents who homeschool their children. They hated that I showed the downside of parents trying to isolate and educate their children at home. Homeschooling is an idyllic situation to them, and many families make a lot of sacrifices to make homeschooling possible. Like missionaries, they want the world to see only the benefits and to join them in their crusade. But all proselytizing that I have ever encountered by passionate people never reveals everything to individuals whom true believers are trying to convert. People in the media eager for a good, quick, emotional story victimize readers and viewers with incomplete and insufficient information that they pawn off as gospel.

But media stereotypes are not consumed only within the borders of the United States. When portraying this country to the outside world in television shows and Hollywood movies, the media again provide a skewed view of what life is like. Foreign visitors and students come to this country with a picture that is far from accurate and have to adjust their impressions once they arrive. One student in Beatrice McKindra's class at Washington High School whose impression of life in the United States was influenced by the media was a young woman named Vanja Selimbegovic. She was a refugee of the 1990s war in Bosnia. She shared an incredible amount of insight about life at Washington High School and in Kansas City, Kan., compared to her war torn homeland. The column I wrote about that encounter ran with the headline **"America not like movies, teen learns."**

Vanja Selimbegovic has worked harder than most students to learn English at Washington High School.

The 15-year-old sophomore had to, because she didn't speak the language when she, her mother, father and 23-year-old sister, Sanja, fled war torn Bosnia. They were among 8,412 Bosnian refugees to arrive in America in 1995 in hopes of having a better future.

Vanja has been in Kansas City, Kan., since Jan. 10, 1996, where she has undergone a rapid Americanization process.

The straight-A student has worked so hard to learn Eng-

lish that she has almost no accent. She did it through reading, practicing and talking with people.

TV also helped. "Just listening to it and looking at it,
you kind of get the point," she said.

Her saying that reminded me of Peter Sodowsky, a kid
from Poland whose family escaped the ravages of communism in that Soviet bloc country during the 1960s. Peter
ended up in eighth grade at the experimental black school
with me. He had said he learned English mostly from
watching television, too.

I always wondered why the school district put that
blond-haired, blue-eyed, very pale white kid in our black
Waring Elementary School. I found out why when I went
to the mostly white Southwest High School in St. Louis.
The high school had mostly gotten over telling racist black
jokes. There were too many black students to permit that
practice to continue. But they told a plethora of Polish
jokes, which were just as racist and painful. Peter would
have been beaten down and wouldn't have stood a chance
of emerging from that system of education as a successful
new American citizen. Being in our black grade school
where we were ignorant of racist jokes against Poles, however, protected him just as Vanja may have been sheltered
in Kansas City, Kan. Generations of other Eastern and
Central European families who had settled in the area
paved the way for her. She might have encountered less
accommodating, accepting circumstances in the Kansas
City area's wealthier suburban communities and schools.

But Vanja has learned that the America she saw in
European movie theaters is nothing like living here.

"I thought it was a lot better than it is," Vanja said.
"Everybody thinks America is a rich country and everybody has money that comes from there.

"But it is not like that. It is not like as they show it in
the movies."

Poverty thrives here, and so does ethnic violence, just as
it does in Bosnia. Vanja described how her peaceful and

fun homeland became dangerous after the 1991 collapse of the Soviet Union. Old hatreds among Serbs, Muslims and Croats boiled into a war that splintered the former Yugoslavian state.

Gunfire and the sound of bombs shattered the safety of Sarajevo, where Vanja lived. Fun family trips to swim at Adriatic Sea beaches disappeared, and so did enjoyable walks through town with friends.

One of the saddest moments was Feb. 2, 1995, when gunfire killed Vanja's best friend at age 16. America had to be better, Vanja thought.

But she found other problems here. Scratching out quality family time is harder in America than it was in Bosnia. Part-time factory work at night keeps her mother busy, and two factory jobs occupy her father.

Vanja also has picked up American teenagers' refrain of being bored with nothing to do. In Bosnia she lived in an apartment building in town, where there were many people and things to do within walking distance. Here, she's in a house that's miles from her peers and teen attractions.

Without a car in America, teenagers are isolated, bored and lonely. "There's just not much to do," Vanja said.

When American teens do get together, Vanja has found that they are louder than young people in Bosnia and tend to show less respect to adults. That's a mistake, she said.

"If they don't respect adults, they won't get that respect themselves," Vanja said. "It's affecting them."

Compared to Bosnia, school here is too easy, she said. Here she has seven classes. In Bosnia she'd be taking 17. Here she has little homework. In Bosnia she'd be overloaded.

But she drives herself to keep learning. "My dream is to continue my education to become something that I can be proud of," Vanja said.

Beatrice McKindra has unshakable faith in Vanja's ability to make that dream come true.

So do I.

Since the start of this Washington High School project, I have sent copies of this series to professors at schools of education and journalism and editors at newspapers to try to show them that there is another way to more comprehensively cover education—by including the many pictures and many-faceted gems that are being created and polished in embattled public schools. But that type of coverage can't be thorough if done by outsiders looking in. The storm clouds of negativity can never be penetrated that way. The positive core of teachers teaching and students learning can be exposed to the public only if the news coverage is from within.

In response to this approach, which I took in my columns, I received nodding support but no sea changes in education coverage from the press. People are slow to go back into urban schools and evaluate the situation in depth, to expose and dispel the many myths and shatter the stereotypes that are relentlessly reinforced in traditional coverage. Change will take time if it ever comes; exposure is required to force a new understanding, which is so desperately needed.

Part II
Chapter 4
The Overlooked and the Neglected

A lot about urban education and students occurs in the shadows. Yet this vast terrain mustn't be ignored. The everyday and often problematic situations affect students' ability to be successful and teachers' efforts to educate young people.

PORTRAIT:
Dennis Bobbitt

He has lived America's history

When Alice Bennett got me a seat in Dennis Bobbitt's class, she said he represented the future of teaching.

Bennett was right. Bobbitt's path into the profession hasn't been typical. But his 20th century story mirrors America's.

He shared his journey with me over breakfast far from his American government seniors in the Class of 1999 at Washington High School.

Bobbitt was 5 years old when his family joined the post-World War II exodus of African-Americans from the South. A lasting memory for him, though, was sitting in the "colored" balcony at a Georgia theater.

His parents settled in Oakland, Calif. He and his five siblings attended newly integrated schools, and his father eventually got an assembly line job at International Harvester.

Bobbitt graduated from high school in the aftermath of

81

the 1965 Watts riot and the start of another exodus: white flight. College wasn't in the cards for Bobbitt then. He followed America's history, joining other men at the Fremont General Motors plant.

"I wanted a car," he said. "I wanted money in my pocket. I wanted independence."

Marriage came next in 1967 and then the draft and the Vietnam War. He served two years in the Army and returned to the GM plant a changed man.

"It taught me to open my eyes," said Bobbitt, 51. "Race and color mean absolutely nothing when your life is on the line. We all bleed red."

In 1970 his wife, Mary, urged him to go to night school while he worked on the line. In 1983 he got a business degree with a history minor at San Jose State University. Then a new American history lesson hit him.

In 1982 his plant closed. Bobbitt, his wife, and their two sons, Christopher and Jerome, joined a new exodus of autoworkers to GM's Fairfax plant. Bobbitt did hard trim, installing wiring and windows on Buicks, Oldsmobiles, Chevys and Pontiacs.

But America's history kept intruding on Bobbitt. Japanese automakers cut the lock U.S. carmakers thought they had on this market. Survival in the global marketplace dictated more plant closings, work force cuts and more robotics to compete with other companies.

"I could see the transience of autoworkers, the shift from plant to plant to plant," said Bobbitt, who ended up at a GM plant in Ohio. "I knew education was going to be very important if I was going to take control of my life."

Like a lot of baby boomers, he went back to college and got a bachelor's degree in education from Mid-America Nazarene College. After 28 years on the GM assembly line Bobbitt took early retirement in 1994. He started teaching social studies that fall at Washington High.

"I was scared," he said. "It's different training kids as opposed to training autoworkers. You're responsible for getting students prepared for life. You fail these kids, and you fail society."

The needs of today's students also are profound. The students are part of America's new history, too, of desegregation, urban blight, single-parent homes and poverty.

They struggle to stay focused, and teachers like Bobbitt in urban public schools struggle to educate them.

Bobbitt has learned that teaching is more than just a job, more than punching a clock and working the line.

It's our new history of rebuilding our youth and America's future.

I found fairly early in my studies at Washington High School that students today are caught in the swirl of inner city life while actively living and pursuing the good. Many times, even when adversity and heartache come their way, they show a tremendous ability to overcome troubles and turn their energies to positive activities and attitudes. I watched the students at Washington High School perform in music, in athletics, saw them at work at their jobs and witnessed their community involvement. Their approach to whatever they did showed commitment, enthusiasm and a growing maturity as they progressed toward graduation. I wrote about the dedication one young man felt for his job in a column headlined, **"Teenager has fun as Barney."**

Barney let me walk with him one Saturday at the Indian Springs Shopping Center in Kansas City, Kan.

TV's friendliest dinosaur is actually a 14-year-old student at Washington High School.

This Barney helped me see that teens care about their community. He works his purple heart out to be kind and attract people to the Kansas City, Kan., mall.

He's a natural at making hordes of little kids happy. "I'm trying to be as much like Barney as possible," he said.

He gets a kick out of filling the 6-foot dinosaur's big purple shoes. Mall-goers look for Barney to give their kids the thrill of meeting the lovable character they see on public television.

"People will ask, 'Is he going to be around today?'" said Rita Slavens, mall spokeswoman. "They like to see him."

But don't expect this Barney to talk or sing his theme song, "I love you, you love me ... ."

He communicates with the kids using only his perpetual smile and body language as he lumbers around the mall, shaking hands, waving to people and hugging dozens of children. "They ask me if I talk, and most of the parents tell them I have a sore throat or something," Barney said.

Barney let me carry the green, helium-filled balloons that he gave to children throughout the mall. I handed one to Andrea Manlove, 9, but she was more interested in shaking Barney's purple hand and looking into his big laughing eyes.

"I like his songs, and I think he's fun," Andrea said.

A few big footfalls down the mall Amanda Zobkiw, 7, hugged Barney. "He's a wonderful person, isn't he?" she said.

Breanna, 6, and Nevada, 7, ran to Barney and hugged the moving carpet.

"I usually get rushed like that," said Barney, who often listens and then turns around when he hears little feet running toward him. It was clear from watching him work that the teen gets a lot more from playing Barney than the $4.75 an hour that he's paid.

He gets to see a world of emotions that the TV character generates in people, ranging from contempt in some teenagers, to fear in toddlers, to unconditional love in kids ages 3 to 10.

"I like making the kids happy," he said. "That's probably the main reason I do it is for the kids."

Barney smiles when toddlers pull back in fear as if they're visiting Santa Claus for the first time. He sweats in the hot costume when teens get abusive and rough.

Barney said it hurts younger kids' feelings when teens say: "'You're not Barney. You're a fake.' Or 'You're extinct down here' or something else dumb.

"They'll push me or they'll say, 'Let's go beat up Barney,'" he said. Once Barney almost got shoved down the escalator.

"You can't move around too well in the costume to defend yourself," Barney said. The purple tail, the hollow, oversized head and all of that padding get in the way.

To sidestep conflicts with teenagers, Barney changed his hours, carries a walkie-talkie piped into security at the mall and keeps his identity a secret. He likes the incognito part and works hard to keep the real person inside the stifling hot purple and green suit a mystery to people at his school and at the mall.

"I think it's kind of fun that way," Barney said. "This way it's like Batman or Spiderman because nobody knows who I am.

"Instead of fighting bad guys, I'm making people happy."

Real-life superheroes don't get any better than that.

By 1999 the student inside that Barney outfit was judged by Alice Bennett, Beatrice McKindra, Scott Milkowart and Dennis Bobbitt to be one of the four winners of the scholarships I provided to the Class of 1999 from money that people who followed the Washington High School series donated to help the top community-minded students go to college. This teen also showed great courage when faced with the disdain of other teens toward his job because he was committed to contributing to his community by "making people happy." That kind of positive drive was a thread that held together many parts of students' lives as they struggled with the unraveling of other parts. That sense of coping and overcoming surfaced in a column I wrote headlined, **"A feeling that stress stalks you."**

A corporate vice president I'd met described with disbelief what she'd seen on TV: A teenager interviewed for a news story on smoking said she puffed to "relieve stress."

"Stress!? What do kids know about stress?" the executive barked. "They've got no stress in their lives!"

I listened, but what she said just didn't seem right. I could identify with her stress because we were the same age.

But it had been years since we were teenagers. The students in Bennett's classes helped me understand that young people feel an ungodly amount of stress, too.

They said students' stress differs from executives'. In many ways, it's worse.

Marcus Harris, 15, said parents' fights create stress for students. "They might grow up and be like that," he said.

Monai Myers, 15, said: "When you're at home and they argue, it reflects on you at school. Some kids can't think. They think about what's going on at home."

Alex Chapman, 15, defined stress as the expectations of teachers, parents and grandparents. "Everybody wants you to succeed in something," he said.

Corey Brinton, 14, said fights at school cause kids stress.

Bobby Ford, 15, agreed, saying upperclassmen create stress by threatening freshmen. Students never know whether it will be enforced with a knife or gun.

"If somebody threatens you, you don't know what they are going to do," said Frank Ollie, 15. "You don't know what they've got."

The FBI reported that violent crime overall had fallen but that arrests of teens under 18 had jumped 7 percent. The number of kids under 18 arrested for murder rose 158.3 percent from 1985 through 1994.

Bennett's kids live where homicides last year hit an all-time high of 70, despite a nationwide trend of murders declining.

Corey raised her hand with one more source of stress. "Boys!" she said. It comes down to whom girls will date.

But peer pressure is on both genders to have sex, Bobby said.

Markesha Clark, 14, Shirley Stewart, 15, and Corey said it weighed more heavily on girls. "If you don't do what the dudes want you to do, they come back to school talking about you," Shirley said.

That raises worries of teen pregnancy. "You're not old enough to be taking care of babies," Bobby said.

Teens today also worry about AIDS, which didn't exist when I was in school. Half the class said they were feeling the stress and coping with it at the right age. The other half said it was robbing them of the carefree fun they should be enjoying in their adolescence.

Drugs become a way out for some kids. A recent study showed that teen drug use is up. Bennett's classes said rising teen stress—discounted by adults—may be the cause.

Alex blamed the media for stressing out black teens. Stories citing higher rates of homicides, incarceration, teen pregnancy, single-parent homes, dropout rates and lower life expectancy keep him worried.

"That's putting black males down," Alex said. "It's more expectations causing you more stress."

Markesha retorted: "But you've got to make them look stupid. Prove them wrong! As a whole group or as one, we've just got to get our act together and prove them wrong."

It's a battle worth fighting, but that's stressful, too.

One of the stresses the students didn't mention then was the problem of not being heard. That discussion went public in a column I wrote headlined, **"Integration broadens horizons."** The question of busing to integrate schools was important to Bennett's students, because Washington High School is such a multicultural

mix of students. It's radically different from the all-white enrollment that existed when the building opened in 1932 as Washington Rural High School in its own little country school district. But
the annexation of that district and the community and the desegregation order imposed in the 1970s by the courts on the Kansas
City, Kan., School District changed that so that white, black, Hispanic, Asian American and Native American students were all
well-represented in the census of the school. The students' reactions to a proposed rollback of integration was fascinating.

Amber Cantrell said something that made me feel welcomed again in Room 43 at Washington High School.

"Hey, that dude from *The Star* is back!" the 14-year-old
blurted out as she entered one of Bennett's classes and
shook my hand.

We've studied Shakespeare, modern literature and well-
known authors. But I wanted to know their thoughts on a
new history and drama being written in the Kansas City,
Kan., School District toward ending busing to integrate
schools.

It's worth exploring during Black History Month because the new plan in Kansas City, Kan., is likely to play
out in Kansas City, St. Louis and other major metropolitan
school districts nationwide. What's sad is that no one has
asked the students what they think about the changes that
could affect them.

They're smart and they know that taking the wheels off
integration programs to revert to neighborhood schools is
likely to resegregate schools and wall off their exposure to
other people. The yo-yo effect of living progressively only
to return to patterns that existed before she was born angered Amber.

"It feels like we're pulled in different directions," she
said.

De'Angello Hillmon, 14, had questions about what
school he'd attend and how he'd get there. No one in class
knew.

Students also expressed a sense of hopelessness over changes that will affect people like them. "It's not like you can stop what's going on," said Sarah Finney, 14.

The Kansas City, Kan., Board of Education adopted a plan recently to end busing for elementary school children to achieve racial balance. It will affect about 330 of the district's 9,700 students currently bused, said Carroll Macke, school district spokesman.

The plan isn't expected to be rolled out until the 1997-98 school year, but it's a start toward ending the 18-year-old U.S. District Court desegregation order in the 23,000-student school system, officials said.

Busing for integration is foreign to people my age and older who went to school decades ago when such great notions were either laughable or only a civil rights dream. But for Bennett's kids, riding big yellow school buses has been a way of life.

"This is all these kids have ever known," Bennett said. "They've not known what it's like to go to neighborhood schools."

Washington High School, with 1,218 students, is 60.18 percent black, 35.8 percent white and 3.53 percent Hispanic, Macke said. Students are bused to Washington High School as part of the desegregation program.

But the school is in a mostly white neighborhood. Busing in that regard has broadened students' circles of friends and built multiculturalism into their educational experience. Keeping up can be challenging, but the different exposure benefits students in the long run, said Neosha Collier, 14.

"Blacks and whites need to be together because they have to learn to work together," she said. "We need to be with other colors to see how other people feel."

That was among the dreams behind having students board buses to desegregate schools. Unfortunately adults don't have as much interest as the students in recognizing the benefits and continuing the forward motion.

The court-ordered desegregation case began in the 1970s and ended in the 1990s. The students adjust as they always have to society's tectonic changes.

Other pressures, however, pop up again and again in teenagers' lives. One of the situations that causes problems and which was recognized by the students in an earlier column is teenage pregnancy. A student in one of Bennett's classes was struggling against her peers and herself. My column on the events was headlined **"Life again cuts in on learning."**

A commotion stirred in Alice Bennett's class, distracting students from essays they had to write on today's heroes.

I tried to ignore it and concentrate on listening and taking notes. But I soon realized that the drama worth noting was between one 14-year-old girl and some boys. The boys teased her but she dissed them right back.

It centered on the girl missing school to have a baby. She returned about two weeks later, after one of the shortest maternity leaves I have ever seen.

But the girl liked school and feared missing too much. Having a new mom in the class, however, adds to Bennett's challenges.

Bennett must constantly weigh the emotional trauma her students face in and outside class against what she can get them to learn in school. Sometimes that's a crapshoot with odds as long as those at The Woodlands racetrack in Kansas City, Kan., which I pass on the way to the school each week.

Education shouldn't be such a gamble. It is, however, when pitted against the distractions of parties, dating and sex, which promise glamour and fun but deliver heartache. Bennett worries about her new mom.

"I'm very happy she's healthy and the baby's healthy," Bennett said. "She's a brave girl and she doesn't back off."

"But it brings up a lot of mixed feelings. A lot of harsh things can happen here."

Not long after her return to class the boys teased the girl about her weight, her body, her gender and her sexuality. But they weren't trying to hurt her.

The boys used humor to mask their curiosity and the awe they felt over someone their age giving birth to a boy like them. In an earlier class we'd discussed why parents have kids.

Megan Randle, 15, said it's because "they want somebody to look like them."

Adrian Hutson, 15, added that it's "so they can try to be like the rest of the world and have a family."

But sometimes babies are conceived accidentally, and young people, including an entire class, must deal with the results. The girls' reaction to the new mom has been as intriguing as the boys'.

The girl had been the center of attention when she was pregnant. But that cooled after the baby was born in January.

It was as if the birth had put distance between them and her because the girl was a mom now, and they all had to adjust. That's raised a tornado of peer pressure, letting me know that teens still feel anger, frustration, confusion and even shame.

Only a stone could sit in class and not care. So when the boys teased the girl I drew some of their fire by asking to see the students' hero essays. But I felt bad about not doing more.

Time has settled the tempest. The girl and I talked about how wonderful it was when her baby started sleeping through the night. "I'm so happy!" she said.

She talked of hope, school and getting a summer job. I gave the girl the name and number of a friend who's now a well-respected executive who had also been a teenage mom growing up in Kansas City, Kan.

My friend finished high school and college and became somebody. She wanted to let the girl know that with hard work and guidance the girl could be somebody, too.

This whole experience has added volumes to what I've learned in Bennett's class.

During the four years I was at Washington High School, I came face to face with many of the problems today's teens struggle with. As I highlighted in a cautionary column headlined, **"Youths face so many distractions that undermine schooling,"**

Teens dropped out of school and vanished from classes. Others got into awful binds.

One got into a gang and was trying to get out. A girl got pregnant, and another was busted in a sex act at school.

A boy was trying to stop committing burglaries. A girl was getting over the suicide of a friend. A boy last week mourned the shooting death of his pal, Jimmy Hinkle, 15. Too many teens weren't troubled with F grades.

These are all good kids, too, but some lost that "good" ID in the shadows of consequences and wrong choices.

The pressures are real, the problems often traumatic, and they should be acknowledged and addressed. As it turns out, contrary to what the company vice president I mentioned earlier said, kids know a lot about stress. But in the same column cited above, I noted that

Teenagers today are like adolescents throughout time.

They're discovering themselves, rebelling against older people and becoming conscious of their surroundings. They talk about the same things: parents, transportation woes, sports, weekend fun, money, jobs, school, summer vacation and the opposite sex.

One event demonstrated to me that young people today march through life following the same path with roughly the same steps as previous generations have. I had broken away from a family vacation to go to the Kansas City Zoo with Alice Bennett's ninth-grade class. The day started with rain. When that ended, the long walk through the zoo was just muggy and hot. The IMAX Theater brought relief. But the thing I remember most was the late morning walk back to the school buses. I had seen many of these young students jump in puddles at the beginning of their freshman year on walks to class. But these older kids now walked around the water, establishing a new, more mature pattern of how they governed their lives.

That new maturity seemed to have taken hold as the students and I began our sophomore year in Beatrice McKindra's class. Going back to school started with a column I did headlined, **"Learning the lessons of the ages."**

A lot of familiar faces, hands and voices have welcomed me back to Washington High School in Kansas City, Kan.

Starting Nov. 2, 1995, I'd spent a lot of time in Room 43 in Alice Bennett's freshman English. With Bennett's help, I returned Oct. 17 to a seat in Room 38 in Beatrice McKindra's sophomore English class.

My hope is to stay with the students I'd met last year, get to know more of them and follow the personal and academic development of the Class of 1999 until they graduate. Their class will be the last one at the school in the 1900s.

That makes these students unique, and they've already shared many special things in their lives with me each time I've returned to McKindra's classes. Markesha Clark showed me her picture, formally outfitted this year for Schlagle High School's homecoming.

Megan Randle proudly pointed out that she'd made the honor roll. Corey Brinton told me about her cute red truck, and Sarah Finney and Natalie Washington always say hello.

I've made a habit of shaking hands with Steve Brown and Joseph Macklin. LeAnna Watson sold me a key chain as part of a yearbook fund-raiser.

After each encounter, and from the sophomores' attentiveness in class, I've noticed something that I didn't see much last year. Bennett said last spring that the summer would bring profound changes.

The students have matured toward becoming responsible men and women in body, mind and spirit. They don't fidget with the nervous energy of children in McKindra's classes as they did in Bennett's.

They dig into the classwork with a commitment to learning that wasn't in many of them a year ago. No one even slept in class when they were reading "Marigolds" by Eugenia Collier, and the students eagerly participated in the discussion, furthering everyone's understanding of the short story.

"There's a growth between the sophomore and the freshmen years," said McKindra, who teaches both grades. "I see that more of them will focus more easily than some of the freshmen."

McKindra makes it easy by connecting life's lessons with the literature. That really surfaced when we read "Marigolds." In it, the main character, Elizabeth, recalls when she was 14 or 15 years old in rural Maryland during the Depression.

Her mother, who was a domestic worker, supported the family. Her father was in tears over being unable to find work.

"The world had lost its boundary lines," the author wrote. "My mother, who was small and soft, was now the strength of the family; my father, who was the rock on which the family had been built, was sobbing like the tiniest child."

Everything was dusty and barren except for a neighbor's marigolds. The little girl in Elizabeth took out her anger at her changing world by destroying the pretty flowers, which mocked reality's harshness. But the budding woman in Elizabeth was ashamed of her actions.

McKindra told her students that their lives were similar to Elizabeth's.

"You want to hold on to childhood because there's security there," she said. "You've got one foot on the line; the other is sliding into adulthood."

When the students returned to Scott Milkowart's class the following year, they spoke of the things taking place in the classes and the rush they were experiencing in being pushed to grow up. That leap toward tomorrow seemed to stand out even more now that they were entering their junior year. I wrote about that sense of maturity in a column headlined, **"Renewing ties to the class of '99."**

Window-size flash units fired in the front of the school auditorium, freezing juniors in mug shots for all time.

A yearbook picture-taking session happened to coincide with my first day back at Washington High School. On Sept. 11, social studies teacher Scott Milkowart allowed me to return with the juniors to a student desk in his American history classes in Room 114.

On my first day back, a loudspeaker ordered juniors go to the auditorium for the picture-taking session. But

Milkowart, who also coaches the football team, managed to get an assignment to his students.

He asked them to write a report on a significant person, issue or event of the 1950s. Milkowart explained his class plan on our walk to the auditorium.

We'll begin in the post-nuclear age and advance into the '70s. That section of American history is closer to what's relevant to today's students.

Milkowart then plans to flash back to the pre-Civil War era and march forward. America's past should connect with the students, giving them and me a mosaic of our shared history.

I found a lot of our shared past in the auditorium, too. I said hello and shook hands with students I'd gotten to know when they were freshmen and sophomores.

It felt good to be welcomed back. I asked the 16- and 17-year-olds to tell me about their summer vacations, and they asked me about mine.

Many told me of special camps they attended, learning to drive, getting new pets, their different jobs, distant travels and boring times at home. Some students still hung out with the same friends.

Others told me that they'd chosen to become loners. Some had become superserious, like Alex Chapman.

I sat with him as the photographers' flashes fired, throwing fleeting shadows against the auditorium walls. Alex had loved to joke around.

"I was clowning for two years," he said. "I can't afford it anymore."

He's pushing himself, shooting for a 3.0 grade point average this year, knowing it's his only hope of getting into college.

I praised Alex and said it was never too late to get serious about school.

Several students had memorized the dates this month when they plan to take the ACT and SAT college entrance exams. The time tunnel to college, adulthood, careers and the rest of their lives isn't dark anymore or nearly as long.

Milkowart reiterated that point throughout the school year when, in addition to history, he lectured the students on the need for maturity, personal responsibility and on how time waits for no one.

The teens' march to maturity was accentuated during one of the longtime traditions of high school that I participated in. I volunteered to be one of the adult chaperones at the Class of 1999 junior prom. It was an elegant affair as most proms are, and I wrote about the experience in a column headlined, **"The night was ruled by dignity."**

Megan Randle carried herself elegantly into the junior and senior prom Saturday night.

I didn't recognize the young lady until the teenager I've known for years at Washington High School said hello. She was among the young women with perfect hair and nails, corsages, rich formal gowns, jewelry, hose and new high-heels.

Many of the young women were escorted by young men in designer tuxedos and loaner shoes with mirror shines. Some of the guys even sported top hats, walking canes and tails.

It was a night to overlook the discomfort of itchy new or rented clothes and focus on just looking good. It was a time to be seen and to check out others in the Grand Ballroom at the Crowne Plaza Hotel.

I watched the show from the check-in table, where I worked with other adult volunteers. They taught me the etiquette of proms, which students religiously followed.

I saw a few of them at last year's prom. I still have the snapshot taken at that big event that Devon Bell gave me of her. She had gone with a group of girls, which is not uncommon these days. A lot more teens in the Class of 1999 attended their junior year with their dates from Washington High and other schools. They all surprised me with their quiet dignity.

They act differently when they're dressed up, said Derrick Hibler, an assistant principal, and Cliff Ferrell, an American government and world geography teacher.

I saw that refinement surface last month at a school ceremony in which about 40 juniors dressed up for their induction into the National Honor Society. They were picked for their character, scholarship, service and leadership. Their parents, teachers and friends in the school auditorium watched with pride, and so did I.

Student dignity and honor also marched around the gymnasium last month at the ROTC awards ceremony. It moved the bleacher crowd and me to tears and standing ovations.

Those events and the prom were a dress rehearsal for what lies ahead. Donnie Mitchell, a world geography and world history teacher, will help them progress when he becomes their senior class sponsor.

"I think it's exciting to see kids get ready to leap from high school," he said. "It's a whole new world."

But that path toward maturity wasn't always filled with refinement and joy. Some students stumbled along the way and those moments might even become near disasters. Jail and prison, for example, eagerly await kids in the urban core, especially those who are African American and Hispanic. The United States has a jail and prison population of about 2.1 million people, more than any other country in the world. According to the National Urban League's State of Black America 2003, "[m]ass incarceration in our society does not affect all Americans equally. It disproportionately targets African Americans and Hispanics. For example, while only 12 percent of the total population, black Americans constitute nearly 50 percent of the prison population. The Sentencing Project, a criminal justice think tank in Washington, D.C., reports that approximately 40% of all black men age 20 to 29 are currently in prison or jail, or on parole or probation. More black males go to jail than to college" (155). The book also states that "[t]he massive scale of imprisonment and the long sentences are having disastrous effects of their own. This includes the creation of a large and embittered population of ex-offenders who return to their communities changed for the worse" (154). These are people whom public education has failed, and that's the biggest crime of all.

I've watched area newspapers and monitored other media as a journalist, and I've been encouraged to see that this ugly trend has not ensnared students I got to know at Washington High School. But one of those students did have a brush with the law while we were both in school. Through what I experienced with him, I also found that the criminal justice system seems to have little regard or respect for poor, low-income, minority kids and the tearful appeals of their families. I wrote about the experience in a column headlined, **"'Good kid' vows he'll go straight."** The waiting room of the Wyandotte County Detention Center, where I went to visit Deaudrey T. MacDonald, was filled with African Americans and Hispanics. That alone was telling, though not surprising considering the statistics cited above. I had trouble getting in to see Deaudrey, and then when I rode the elevator to his floor we could not find a telephone that worked allowing us to hear each other through the thick glass that separated visitors from the uniformed prisoners. We went to visitors' booths on several floors before we found a pair that worked. Also darkly comical, I got turned around on the way out and ended up in an abandoned control room area in the bowels of the jail. Officials at the detention facility were not happy with me. But they also didn't forget that I was there that weekend to visit Deaudrey. It may have worked in his favor. I shudder to think what might have happened if I had not gotten involved.

Deaudrey T. MacDonald's attorney had a curious question: Why does *The Star* care?

Three years of knowing Deaudrey since his freshman year in Alice Bennett's English class at Washington High School made me care enough to visit him Sept. 20 at the Wyandotte County Jail. He was 17 then, in an orange jail jumpsuit and locked up with men.

About a month behind bars had smothered the affable Deaudrey I'd known, leaving a scared kid with a caged look.

Rain fell outside the jail on this Sunday. Basketballs inside the lockup gym pounded. I had even heard the dribbling and the noises of men's raised voices as I walked around the detention center outside looking for an open door and a way in.

"I've been praying a lot," Deaudrey said into a phone because a glass wall separated us. "I've asked God to be my personal savior. He's been keeping me out of harm's way."

Deaudrey was among the 439 freshmen in the Class of 1999 at Washington High School. He explained that he wasn't among the 197 seniors counted last month at Washington High.

He didn't drop out as the 55 percent enrollment plunge might indicate. He had switched to Wyandotte High School.

I had seen his name in *The Kansas City Star* in connection with a car accident involving a police officer. I wrote to Deaudrey in jail to get on his visitors list. I showed up because of our tie to the Class of 1999. Deaudrey was arrested Aug. 3 and charged as an adult with eluding a police officer and as a juvenile with aggravated assault on an officer and criminal damage to property.

He was accused of trying to run over a motorcycle officer after hitting a pole near 79th Street and Leavenworth Road in Kansas City, Kan. The officer, who was uninjured, fired once as the car sped off.

Blame it on the 1987 silver Chrysler LeBaron that Deaudrey worked two jobs to buy for $1,283. Blame it on too many TV car chases without crushing real-life consequences.

"I was happy to finally get transportation," Deaudrey said. "And then boom. It all went away."

Boom is also what happened the day after my jail visit. Deaudrey was released to house arrest with his grandmother, Lillie Scruggs. Then boom, he was back in school with college dreams again.

Boom, he turned 18, and boom, his attorney, Michael Highland, and the district attorney's office worked out a no-contest plea.

Wyandotte County District Judge R. Wayne Lampson accepted it Friday morning.

"He's a good kid, and he had a good reputation before he got into this," Scruggs told me before the hearing.

On Friday, Deaudrey and I walked into the courthouse together. I told him the last time I'd been in the building was as a reporter the year he was born.

"This is all new to me," Deaudrey nervously replied.

"He seems to be a really good kid," said Vicki Meyer, an assistant district attorney and a Kansas City, Kan., school board member. Deaudrey had stayed out of the justice system until the plea on the juvenile charge of aggravated assault.

Probation will be his likely sentence. But if he messes up again, he could serve prison time as an adult, Meyer said.

Lampson told Deaudrey that a slip-up could cost him more than 7½ years and a $100,000 fine. That would put him in one of the prisons that I've visited in Kansas. I had described those encounters to him and other students when they were freshmen.

That's not going to happen, Deaudrey told me.

"Being in jail between walls will make you crazy," he said. "You feel like a caged animal."

Deaudrey, who's been in an anti-gun, anti-violence group at school, insists that he has grown from his bad experience. "It brought me wisdom," he said.

"I was not responsible," he said. "Not being responsible can take you a long way.

"It can get you into some places where you really don't want to go. I have to be more responsible for my actions."

We shook hands after his plea, just as we always had at Washington High. I pray that others learn from his experience.

Deaudrey did graduate from Wyandotte High School and enrolled at Donnelly College in Kansas City, Kan. We remain in touch.

Deaudrey stumbled but was able to catch himself before he fell to his knees. Other students don't stumble but get pushed by events beyond their control. Christopher Thoele, for example, was propelled into adulthood by an event that took place in the summer of 1997. When I spoke to him after school started in the fall, he said he'd had to grow up in a flash to help his family meet new responsibilities and challenges after his father died. Jennifer Rogers was forced to face a different life-changing tragedy when her family's house was heavily damaged by fire. I wrote about her struggles and how she managed to cope with the new challenges in a column I did headlined, **"Fire offers hard lesson in faith."**

Sometimes the heavy dramas of life get in the way of learning at Washington High School in Kansas City, Kan.

It prompted Jennifer Rogers to turn around in her desk and ask me a tough question this week in Dennis Bobbitt's American government class. "Do you believe in God?" she said after I gave her back her smoke-damaged senior memory book which she had shared with me.

The smoke was from a fire. She had told me about that last week. The book with her many priceless photos and keepsakes was among the few things she salvaged from the blaze, which left her family homeless.

Learning how such tragedies deeply affect students has been part of studying with the Class of 1999 at Washington High School.

Fire Marshal Robert Rocha said overloaded electrical equipment caused the March 30 fire in the two-story frame house at 1136 N. 32nd St. Flames raced from the kitchen and back porch areas to the second floor before firefighters contained the blaze.

Jennifer, 18, her father, Phillip; mother, Sheri; and sister, Kimberly, 14, escaped unharmed but with few possessions. The American Red Cross in Wyandotte County provided some assistance.

The family is living with relatives and friends until repairs can be made. Fire officials listed the damage at $25,000.

What's worse is the insurance had lapsed. Jennifer's father had been ill and unable to work until recently. Boards now cover the windows and doors on the quaint 87-year-old house that her family had just remodeled with a new roof, interior improvements and siding.

The fire has become an interloper, standing between Jennifer and her dream of being only the second person in her family to graduate from high school and the first to attend college. Giving up isn't an option.

I told her I believe in God. I also told her that faith sometimes is the only thing that steels folks facing great hardships.

She said her mom offered the same counsel. A pastor on Sunday told her mom that perhaps hidden in the rubble of the fire was a blessing.

Jennifer also has wrestled mightily with whether to talk about the tragedy.

"I don't want to bring it to school and cry about it," said Jennifer, who plans to study at Pittsburg State University and become a teacher. "I want to be strong for my family.

"Is it wrong for me to feel bad about my house?"

I told her it was human to mourn the loss of her home and the security it had offered to her since she was 6 years old. It's OK to grieve. Grieving has to occur before healing can begin.

After class last week I went to her home. Tia, the family dog, has singed eyebrows and was barking in back. Fire-damaged appliances filled the back yard, along with a trash bin of debris.

Each signaled progress, muscled together by friends, co-workers and the family in rebuilding the home. "It's devastating to lose everything you have," Phillip Rogers said.

"You see fire trucks going up and down the street," he said. "But you never think too much of it until it's your own home.

"Really it's a hell of a feeling to see flames coming out of your place. But I've raised my kids here. We're not going to give up. We can't."

I know the Rogers will triumph over the tragedy, and Jennifer will make her family proud by graduating May 25 from Washington High.

Because Jennifer shared her story with me, she received a hefty scholarship for college from a faith-based organization. She also received several letters and checks from individuals who wanted her to know that they, too, believed that she would prevail with God's love and guidance.

When kids are faced with such hardships in their young lives, they look for something steadfast, something they can hold onto. In some cases it is their faith that strengthens them, but they also need to know that they can turn to others—their peers or caring adults—to help them through the difficult times. Jennifer turned to me with her concerns, and I am glad I was there that day to offer some semblance of hope to her. But too often we adults won't acknowledge or accept teens' grief or despair over an event in their lives—no matter how important or how (seemingly) trivial. Instead we use the opportunity not to comfort and console, but to lecture and make the episode into a "learning experience." Yet the inevitable "You just don't understand!" that is hurled our way should serve as a warning: when students get caught up in the outcome of bad things we must be compelled to stand with them and help them make sense of their pain rather than teach them a lesson. I wrote about one such instance in a column headlined, **"They fight these tears every day."**

> Last Tuesday, I sat with the students as they grieved at New Fellowship Baptist Church over the shooting death of their classmate, Justin Tyrell Stanley.
>
> It was a moving learning experience for me, and it showed how our young people are traumatized by modern-day urban tragedies.
>
> The service for Justin, 16, was profound on many fronts. Students who've known Justin since grade school filled the church. His comrades in ROTC, including Jeffrey Singleton, served as solemn ushers.
>
> I didn't know Justin. But I attended the service to support and comfort the many students who've welcomed me into their lives. Justin had recently transferred from Washington High to Wyandotte High School.
>
> On Feb. 4, he was sent home for being disruptive. He was shot to death about 3:30 p.m. in a North 38th Street parking lot. A boy, 15, surrendered to police the next day in the shooting.

A white teddy bear rested on Justin's open casket. After all he was just a kid. His classmates sat in somber, respectful silence more than an hour before the service started.

Teenagers aren't supposed to die. Their longtime friends aren't supposed to cry. Yet the church dripped with tears.

Alex Chapman and Bobby Ford let me sit between them in the bolted-down, wooden folding seats. They'd known Justin about a third of their lives. I'd known them since they were freshmen.

Alex and Bobby were much smaller in 1995. In church, I was the little guy sandwiched between two linebacker-sized young men.

It's natural for each new generation to be bigger than the one that came before them. But our promise to future generations also must be greater.

The service made me remember my friend's funeral in 1969. That was during the Vietnam War, and John Henry McSwine was a fallen Marine.

The neighborhood outside the Quindaro Boulevard, Kansas City, Kan., area church, where many of the teenagers live, reminded me of war, too.

Families and youths struggle to maintain their dreams against armies of decay, poverty, government neglect and despair. The numbers of wounded urban kids tracking their pain into schools are too many for educators to treat and teach.

The church heaved and convulsed with great sobs of sadness. Justin's family and friends eulogized him as a high-spirited, religious, fun-loving young man who enjoyed making people laugh.

"Now Justin is at peace with God as his new best friend," one of the teenage speakers said.

That helped his young friends grieve. But the minister, as often happens, upset things by spending too much time lecturing and talking down to the teens about crime, drugs, teen pregnancy, violence and the irresponsible, bad behavior of youth. The time to get that message across should have been sprinkled over the years of the kids' lives and perhaps it would have prevented Justin's untimely death.

The few adults in the pews were enthused by the minister's words. But I watched as many teens stopped shedding healing tears and simply turned off.

After the column ran I received feedback from adults who criticized me for not praising the minister. "Those kids need to hear that," many said. "If not then, when?" The time to counsel should have started when these young people were just beginning to learn the language. That socialization process from parents to children, adults to young people needs to be positively spun and ongoing. It just doesn't stick when it's given as castigation at a time when consoling is the only elixir that will ease the students' heartache and pain.

Part III
Student Portraits

Be open to listening to young people's dreams. Their gift in return will be your ability to dream and have ideals as someone who's young again, too.

*I*n too many people's eyes, teenagers grow into the awful stereotype of being society's problem children. Statistics reported in the news media of teen alcohol and drug use, sex, pregnancy, vandalism, low test scores, dropout rates and violence should serve to tell the community that the needs of young people are not being met. In the best of all possible worlds, adults should redouble efforts, energy and resources to answer the cries of adolescents and meet those concerns. The goal is to have young people grow up to be productive, taxpaying citizens rather than continue to cause problems and be a drain on society. But instead many people add their own bizarre misinterpretation to the university studies and government data. They see teen problems as being hopelessly beyond their ability to offer help. They view the statistics as reinforcing the stereotypes of teenagers being malicious, vicious and incorrigible.

To some extent their perceptions are right. Students can and do take an aggressive stance towards adults, sometimes going to "Jerry Springer"-type extremes. (Chapter 6 highlights this behavior.) Nevertheless, it's unfortunate when adults use these problems as excuses to cocoon themselves and back away from interacting with teens. I witnessed that reluctance at a career day at a high school. A businesswoman who had been invited to the school to talk about her career to students to expose them to her profession was petrified over the prospect of standing in front of what she thought would be a hostile, unappreciative audience. She was only at the school because her manager hadn't given her the option of saying no to the assignment. I assured her that the students wouldn't bite. Most of the time teenagers—just like adults—are warm, interested and accepting, and they ask good questions. But also like adults, they can sense fear on a person and they will react accordingly. They can instinctively tell whether a person is genuine—or "keeping it real," as they say—in talking with them or if the whole presentation is phony. Students, like adults, will shift to an aggressive, protective, reactive mode if they intuitively feel that something is wrong.

I had asked a diversity group at St. Luke's Hospital, in Kansas City, in December 1999 whether I could use a "Star Trek" analogy to explain this concept better. Michael Weaver, a physician at the hospital raised his right hand in a split finger Vulcan sign and said, "Speak!"

I explained that on the many "Star Trek" TV shows it became clear that the starships served two purposes: they and their crews were to explore the galaxy in hopes of charting new courses and discovering new things—"to boldly go where no man has gone before," as the old series used to open. But they also were warships equipped with phazers, photon torpedoes and an energy shield to protect the craft. In addition, these warships had sensors so they could pick up when other vessels, planets or species they encountered were armed for a fight. I explained to the group at the hospital that if people are walking around with their photon torpedoes armed, their phazers ready to fire and their shields up, other people would pick that up and respond in kind. Everyone would go around armed for a fight. No one would be able to beam anything or anyone in or out for exploration, and peaceful missions of discovery wouldn't stand a chance.

That's how teenagers often react to adults' reactions to them. Everyone is at "red alert," a high, tense state of combat readiness because they fear something bad or hurtful is going to be said or happen. They all have their shields up. Everyone is ready to fire off verbal salvos, and when that happens no one is at peace with the mental and emotional ability to explore across bridges that must be open to ensure that transgenerational learning takes place.

It's important that adults step beyond the many stereotypes about teenagers and open themselves to being in their lives. That's what Washington High School taught me. I saw the importance of saying hello to the students whenever and wherever I saw them, going into places where adults don't go often enough and listening to students' concerns as well as their dreams. What I learned about the students strengthened my own conviction that adults *must* keep their own defensive shields down while breaking down the teens' barriers of mistrust and fear.

In this chapter, I present portraits of individual students whom I got to know during my four years at Washington High School. These portraits are meant to illuminate just how valuable connections with young people can be. They are fun to get to know and older people gain from the ideals, energy and purity of thought that young people possess. And the teens need to have people in their lives who can encourage them to go faster, farther and higher rather than give up and fall back settling for mediocrity or less. They need to be encouraged to dream so that they can achieve. Building bridges with teens is good for everyone. *Can't* and *don't* are not options.

PORTRAIT:
Steve Brown and
Joseph Macklin

Basketball's lessons carry over to life

Steve Brown and Joseph Macklin invited me to their game, so I went to see them play at Washington High School.

Steve is 6 feet 3 inches tall and plays center/forward for the Washington Wildcats in Kansas City, Kan. Joseph is 5 feet 11 inches tall and is a guard and co-captain of the team.

Each 16-year-old sophomore began playing varsity basketball as a freshman. I met them back then after I began visiting Alice Bennett's English class Nov. 2, 1995.

Steve and Joseph are sophomores now in Beatrice McKindra's English class. At the game the Wildcats played the Blue Valley Northwest High School Huskies.

Some things hadn't changed since I'd left high school 24 years ago: Students, parents, teachers, coaches and family members filled the bleachers. Cheerleaders for the dueling teams fanned the schools' spirit in the acoustically challenged gym. Some teens I knew in the school band entertained the crowd, and the boys played breathless basketball.

But what's different is that the players aren't dumb jocks. Standards in education have forced them to shake off classmates' confetti showers of cheap adulation and hit the books hard.

Grade requirements of "C" or better make today's athletes play a lot smarter than they did more than a generation ago.

Steve, who has about a 3.0 grade point average, lectured me on his love of and philosophy about the game: "When you're competitive in sports, it makes you work hard in class. So you have to have a work ethic in basketball, and you take that into schoolwork.

"Hard work makes you better in whatever it is. You've got to put school first. For me, basketball is behind school, but not by very much, because I believe basketball is going to pay for my education in college."

Joseph is driven in similar ways to stay in the game.

"If you don't have your grades, you can't play the sport," said Joseph, who has a 3.5 GPA. "If you have a love for the game, you'll do whatever it takes."

Joseph cross-pollinates a philosophy he picked up in choir with basketball, schoolwork and life: "Good, better, best. Never let it rest until your good is your better and your better is your best."

Steve and Joseph also have strong cheerleading camps at home. John Macklin said he is proud of his son, who knows athletics is useless without scholastics. "He's pretty conscientious and pretty mature for his age," Macklin said before the game.

Stephen L. Brown felt the same way about his son, Steve.

"He knows school comes first," Brown said. "I'm a big believer in that.

"Every now and then I get on him. But he takes advice really well."

So their families enable their success.

Joseph and Steve hope that basketball scholarships finance their college education. They also share hoop dreams of playing in the NBA.

But they know they will need to rely on their wits to keep scoring in life. That's why Steve also wants to be an accountant or a lawyer, and Joseph hopes to become a businessman or go into sports medicine.

Steve and Joseph played well against the Huskies, who defeated the scrappy Wildcats 68-59. But in the long game called life, Steve and Joseph will stay high point scorers if they hold on to their winning philosophies and the people who feed them the round ball of success.

PORTRAIT:
Kresha Crift and
Le-Andra R. Hood

Student's hard work pays in A's

Kresha Crift proudly showed me her report card last week at Washington High School.

The 15-year-old sophomore in Beatrice McKindra's English class had been on the "A" honor roll since she was a freshman. Her new grade card with all A's showed that she has maintained that high academic standing.

It seemed odd in this day when dissing school is cool. But Kresha learned long ago that getting good grades matters to students who plan to go to college on scholarships.

She's taught me that schoolwork is still important to high-achieving teens.

Kresha is taking accounting, biology, Spanish, health, algebra, sewing and English. What's wonderful is she likes all of her courses because each has something different to teach.

"I admire her," McKindra said. "She works well with other people.

"She's almost ideal, really."

But that winning attitude didn't blossom overnight. Over the last 12 years, Kresha has developed systems for success.

One of what I call Kresha's "academic enablers" is her friend Le-Andra R. Hood, a 14-year-old freshman. They have been best friends since preschool, and each A-student pushes the other to succeed.

Le-Andra said she is drawn to Kresha's positive attitude, sage counsel, wisdom and sense of humor. Theirs is a small but important support group. It will help Kresha reach her dream of becoming a nurse, accountant or computer engineer and help Le-Andra become a criminal lawyer.

"It seems like we're leading each other and following each other at the same time," Kresha said.

Another academic enabler is Kresha's mom, Lois A. Stone. The 45-year-old beautician recently earned a bachelor's degree in human services at St. Mary College.

Kresha said her mom is her mentor and role model. "I really feel good about her," Kresha said.

But she also remembers Stone riding her about doing homework early and stressing the importance of good grades. Stone remembers, too, especially when Kresha brought home low marks back in first grade.

That was unacceptable, and Stone worked hard with Kresha to teach her good study habits and to pull up those low marks.

"In the long run, it really has helped me out a lot," Kresha said.

Stone sees Kresha as her friend, and they maintain open mother-daughter chat lines about success and life.

Schools must be academic enablers, too. "I think sometimes students like Kresha are not appreciated," McKindra said.

"I try to tell them when they are doing a good job," McKindra said. "But sometimes I think we lose sight of them because we have to deal with the loudmouths who want attention for negative things.

"We as teachers have to deal with them more than someone like Kresha. I think we need to change that."

Meanwhile, students like Kresha work to keep their focus and a winning philosophy about school. "I think of school as going to work," Kresha said.

"When you go to work you have to be on time, and you have to be prepared," she said. "I think of the teacher as the boss and the assignments they give as work assignments."

Kresha said she's found that the more time and energy she put into her work, the bigger the payday in grades.

Her strong work ethic today will keep paying her dividends now and in the future.

PORTRAIT:
Sarah E. Finney and
Corey Brinton

Students also learn in pools, gym

Sarah E. Finney ran toward me with her arms open when she saw that I actually showed up to see her perform at Washington High School.

But she stopped short of an embrace. "I'd hug you, but I'd get you all wet," said Sarah, who was wearing a swimsuit. We laughed when I said a handshake would do.

She and Corey Brinton had invited me to their recent swim meet at Washington High School in Kansas City, Kan. I got to know them the previous year when they were freshmen in Alice Bennett's English class.

They're sophomores now in Beatrice McKindra's English class.

Seeing Sarah and Corey swim for the SabreCats against the St. Pius X Warriors was my effort to devote as much time to the girls' extracurricular interests as to the guys' in the Class of 1999. I was surprised to see that the Washington, Sumner and Schlagle SabreCats included other sophomores I knew, such as Sara Hampton and Michelle Hyde.

A crowd gathered to watch the SabreCats, including some of McKindra's other students, such as William Hawkins, Devon Bell and Tiauda M. Taylor.

The Olympics in 1996 showed the growing popularity of women's sports. Girls' high school athletic programs are riding that wave, too. What also was clear at poolside was that girls benefit as much from sports competition as boys do.

Kansas lawmakers who drew fire this year for attacks on extracurricular student activities obviously failed to check out the games, the music performances and swim meets. They would have seen students having fun, supporting each other through positive peer pressure and growing as people through that involvement.

Sarah said participating in swimming, track, band, Close-Up, French Club and ROTC gave her a better perspective on life. The subjects motivate her academically, and she hopes they'll help her get into college.

"When you do sports, you're getting an education," she said. School for some students wouldn't be worth attending without the extracurriculars.

McKindra said teachers had noted the attention shift from fields of study to fields of play. That's why some use the extracurriculars as carrots to drive students toward academics.

Corey said swimming and singing in the SongCats choral group helped define who she is. "It's my life," she said.

Corey said they gave her an inner drive, which she channeled into her schoolwork.

"I think the music, the arts, basketball, swimming, track ... it's there to help us expand our world," Corey said.

Julie Brinton, Corey's mom; Susan Findley, Sarah's mom; and Washington Principal Larry A. Englebrick, who watched the swim meet with me, agreed. Students get interpersonal skills and learn from each other.

"The kids actually have to work together to figure things out together," Englebrick said.

Jennifer Anderson, an assistant swim coach and algebra teacher, likes being part of the process. "It's a good chance to get to know the kids better and to see them in a different atmosphere and in another way they can be successful," she said.

When the meet was over and the score showed that the SabreCats had won, the girls got together, picked up Anderson and threw her—clothes, shoes and all—into the pool. I was relieved that their teamwork focused on her instead of me.

PORTRAIT:
Courtney G. Bettis

First steps on the road to dreams

Courtney G. Bettis shared her dream with me three years ago. She was a freshman in Alice Bennett's English class at Washington High School.

Last school year, Courtney was in Beatrice McKindra's sophomore English class, and so was I. This year, we're in Scott Milkowart's American history class for juniors, where Courtney's dream remains alive.

The honor roll student took the ACT exam this month in her journey to be a lawyer.

"I felt like I could help people," Courtney, 17, said. "I felt like I could bring justice."

Her dream is worth sharing during Black History Month. Courtney wants to study law at Howard University.

"My ultimate goal is to become a judge," she said. "My biggest goal is to be a Supreme Court justice."

"Maybe one day I'll get there."

It's been done before. Kathy Jenkins, with a Howard University research center, said one of the law school's most famous graduates was Thurgood Marshall. He served 23 years as chief counsel for the NAACP.

He took an injustice in Courtney's home state to the Supreme Court. That 1954 Brown vs. Topeka Board of Education ruling outlawed legal segregation.

President Lyndon B. Johnson in 1967 appointed Marshall as the first African-American justice on the Supreme Court. Marshall retired in 1991 and died in January 1993.

Courtney wants to be like him. But television was what turned her on to law. She started watching "L.A. Law" when she was about 5 and became hooked on the show and the legal profession.

"It's something that she has always wanted to do," said Roderick Bettis, Courtney's father. "She sets goals for herself, and she reads a lot.

"I think that contributed to her having high ambitions."

Milkowart praised Courtney and her parents, Roderick and Anita Bettis. "She's a good kid, a good student with a nice demeanor," Milkowart said.

As Courtney grew from a girl to a young woman, she kept strengthening herself academically and emotionally to capture her dream. Going to a black college is part of how she plans to shape herself for greatness.

Howard University is one of 103 historically black colleges and universities. It was established in 1867 and named after Gen. Oliver O. Howard, a hero of the Civil War, which Courtney's class is studying this month. It is among the oldest and most prestigious among black universities. It was set up to help African-Americans earn college degrees when white schools wouldn't admit blacks.

Historically black colleges and universities continue to meet a need, said Michelle Green with the United Negro College Fund. Howard University gets federal money and is not a member of UNCF.

But at the 39 UNCF member schools, 34 percent of the students come from families with gross incomes of less than $25,000. About 85 percent of the students need financial aid and 40 percent are the first in their families to go to college.

"Typically at a historically black college the class sizes are a lot smaller, there is a lower student-to-teacher ratio and there is more nurturing and mentoring that goes on," Green said.

Universities like Howard keep doors open in this era of anti-affirmative action efforts, which close opportunities to minorities. I pray that Courtney's dreams come true and that others like her dare to dream, too.

PORTRAIT:
Michael and Marcus Harris

A pair sharing strengths

After Marcus Harris won his wrestling match, he left the mat and hugged his brother Michael.

Michael was just as eager to compete and win at the Wyandotte County Wrestling Championships. I've found the identical twins to possess a wonderful combo spirit and drive for success.

I saw that in their freshman year, when I first began observing their class. They've reinforced the feeling with strong handshakes, good schoolwork and upbeat conversations each year.

Both are juniors now in Scott Milkowart's American history classes. "They want to do well, and they steer away from trouble," Milkowart said.

I went to see Michael and Marcus play football, and last month I saw them wrestle at Piper High School. Semifinal victories allowed each to advance to the state competition last weekend in Wichita. Both wrestled well, but neither placed.

While I waited to see Michael wrestle in the 189-pound competition, Marcus took a seat near me in the bleachers. I congratulated him on his victory, and I told him I hadn't seen real wrestling since I was in high school 25 years ago.

"Is it about the same?" he asked of the "olden days."

I laughed, saying it was as good if not better. All around us, guys from the competing schools practiced moves, worked out with jump ropes or watched teammates struggle for a pin.

It's an ancient, pure sport. Cave drawings and carvings in France dating back 20,000 years show wrestlers in holds and leverage positions.

Egyptian art shows wrestling dating from 2,500 B.C. The Greek poet Homer wrote about it, and the philosopher Plato was among the many stars and advocates of the sport, which marries mind, body and spirit.

Michael and Marcus, 17, said football, wrestling and track kept them focused on doing well in school, where they're B students. "I feel that just sitting around, it's not going to do anything for me," Marcus said.

He's hoping for an athletic scholarship to pay his way through college and into a teaching career. Few people in his family have gone to college. "I want to be the next one to step up," Marcus said.

Michael said he hoped sports would open a gateway to a better future for him. "They help me as life goes on," he said.

"I want to do something good in life," said Michael, who hopes an athletic scholarship will enable him to become an engineer. He credits their grandmother, who died last year, and their mother for pushing them to constantly do better.

"They always told us, 'You boys have a chance in life,'" Michael said.

Their mother, Sandra K. Harris, said her pride in Marcus, Michael, her daughter, Jessica Holloway, 12, and stepson, JuJuan Miller, 22, is unending.

"I think the world of them," she said of her twins. "No matter where I go in school, I get compliments on them. It lets me know I have done something."

Each twin also admires and supports the other. "I look up to him because he also has done some great things," Michael said. To them, family is extremely important.

When we first met in 1995, they were wearing T-shirts from their family reunion. It's an annual gathering of more than 100 people from throughout the country. This year their family members, who are black, white and Hispanic, will get together in Kansas City, Kan.

"When I see that many people come together, it just looks like one big, happy world," Marcus said.

That spirit and vision will carry Marcus and Michael far.

PORTRAIT:
Natalie Washington

Attitude makes music even sweeter

The polished ebony finish in the Yamaha piano caught Natalie Washington's rocking reflection as her fingers deftly played a romantic classical song.

Framed pictures of African-American music legends, including Lena Horne, Bessie Smith, Scott Joplin, Sarah Vaughan and Josephine Baker, seemed to smile as Natalie played in the Kansas City, Kan., home of her instructor, Lorraine Peery Long. I had met Natalie there on a recent Saturday to applaud the things she does outside of class.

Helen R. Washington, Natalie's mother, sat on the living room couch with me, where we enjoyed the performance. Long's keen, discerning ear and critique ensured that Natalie's good work will only get better.

Natalie's music lesson helped me see how students like her also learn from wonderful teachers outside of school and how caring parents like Washington nurture and support the process. I got turned on to this extrasensory treasure when an office loudspeaker announcement interrupted Scott Milkowart's American history class.

The announcement congratulated Natalie on winning a prestigious music award.

I had studied with her since she was a freshman in the Class of 1999. She has always said hello and other nice things but never mentioned a word about her special talents.

Natalie, 16, has sung alto in the Washington "SongCats" since she was a freshman and has traveled to Atlanta and Toronto to perform. This year, the group is going to New York.

"It's real fun," she said. "You get to see a lot of different things and meet different people."

Natalie just returned Saturday with about 50 students from a chaperoned spring break bus tour of 12 historically black colleges. The Beta Lambda Chapter of Alpha Phi Alpha Fraternity Inc. sponsored the trip. It allowed Natalie to see Florida A&M University, where she hopes to go to college.

Milkowart can see that happening. "She has a really good learning attitude," he said.

That learning attitude filled Long's home with Natalie's music. On the wall was a surreal piece of art that said, "Music Gives Wings to the Mind and Flight to the Imagination."

Piano performances outside of school take her to high notes of success. Natalie's mother opened a scrapbook, showing me the Kansas State High School Activities Association certificates for Natalie's prize-winning work.

"It has kept her busy and given her direction in life," Washington said.

Long added, "She has played as well as anybody on a national and international scale."

For Natalie, music is a lovely dimension of life outside of home, church and school.

"The people in the music department are outgoing and involved in different things at school, and they are the ones who don't get into trouble with the teachers and faculty," Natalie said.

She said music kept her occupied and focused. Recent studies have shown that students who play the piano do better in school. Researchers found that children scored higher on tests of the reasoning required for science and math.

Natalie has been on the honor roll every year. "I know in the end all of my hard work will pay off when I am ready to go to college," she said.

After she graduates, Natalie plans to seek college degrees in either music, computer science or business administration.

"She works hard, and she has a lot of perseverance," Long said.

Those are wonderful, life-enhancing qualities that young people like Natalie continue to impress me with at Washington High School.

PORTRAIT:
Jerry Cheray

Marching to a new drummer

Jerry Cheray knelt behind a video camera in an aisle of the auditorium at Washington High School.

When students began their forensics performances, Jerry caught each act on tape.

A few months ago, I'd paid to see the school performance of "The Wiz," in which Jerry handled props. So I couldn't resist buying a ticket from his classmate, Michelle Hyde, and staying after Scott Milkowart's American history to see the recent forensics show.

I thought, as I watched Jerry work, that someday he'll rerun the tape of his life and be amazed by the drama. Jerry's story, like the Reconstruction era that Milkowart tested his students on this week, is a personal struggle of a 16-year-old rebuilding himself from near tragedy.

No one would know it now. The three-year ROTC vet will be among 120 clean-cut cadets I'll see Thursday night in the school gym at an ROTC awards banquet. Jerry had shared the story of his rebound with me after Christmas break.

"I've seen him up and down," said Jerry's ROTC instructor, retired Air Force Lt. Col. Rick McKee. "Right now, he's more up. He's on our drill team and tries desperately to do good."

Call it the lure of the streets in a city with few jobs, poor mass transit and little to offer kids. Drugs, alcohol, sex, crime, gangs and violence sing their siren songs. I've seen the headlines of wrecked teenage lives. But Jerry knew some of the stars of those tragedies.

He also was on his way to becoming one of them. But Christmas was his time to heal and rebuild. He'd be moved from Washington to Wyandotte High if he didn't.

"It was meant to wake me up," he said.

He went straight, but one of his ROTC comrades didn't. An angry incident forced Justin T. Stanley out of Washington and into Wyandotte High School.

On Feb. 4, his first day at Wyandotte, Justin was sent home about noon for being disruptive. He was shot to death about three hours later by another teen in a parking lot. Justin's tragedy may have helped save the lives of Jerry and countless others.

The next day at Washington High, I watched Jerry help make "The Wiz" come to life. It's a play about a Kansas kid swept up in a twister and dropped in a place called Oz. She met good people who helped her, but there was a witch who wanted her dead.

The good people outnumbered the bad in "The Wiz." They do, too, at Washington High, where the marquee reads, "There is no progress without struggle.' I always like reading and jotting down the uplifting messages on the marquee. Dorothy made it back to Kansas, and Jerry has gone straight.

"I think he's making a better effort in class," Milkowart said. "It's a start."

Jerry's mother, Sharon Coppinger, is encouraged, too: "I am very proud of him for what he has done and how he has turned his life around."

Jerry's plans include graduating from high school, spending two years in the Kansas National Guard and joining the Navy.

"I've only been in Kansas and Missouri," he said. 'I want to go across the sea. I want to explore the world."

Jerry said discipline in the ROTC and the color guard helped turn him around.

"Very few people we deal with initially have a whole lot of structure in their lives," McKee said. ROTC teaches teens the value of the uniform, the importance of showing respect, saying 'yes sir' and 'no sir,' proper grooming, punctuality, good grades and marching.

Jerry is marching to the beat of a drummer now who wants to see him have a future worlds beyond Washington High School.

PORTRAIT:
Sarah E. Enright

Hair affair brings out true colors

Black and white yearbook pictures fail to tell the colorful story of Sarah E. Enright's time at Washington High School.

I met her last year when she was a junior. I saw her again this summer at the West Wyandotte library, where she likes to read and study.

We talked before this school year started about her uniqueness, which *The Hatchet* yearbook may never capture. Filling in the gaps is one of the joys I get from studying with the Class of 1999. Sarah is a class stand-out—mostly because of her hair.

It's long and straight. But at different times she'll color it blonde, pink, red, green, purple or blue. It's purple today. But soon she'll change it to blue.

"I do love blue," Sarah said. "It makes me feel really vibrant, up and alive. It makes me want to do things.

"Purple? I like that, too. It makes me feel really good about myself. Red and pink are really good, but they don't make me feel as good as blue does."

The 18-year-old Kansas City, Kan., woman also dresses in baggy, mod clothes that she buys mostly in Westport. She's had her earlobes stretched at a shop on Troost Avenue. Sarah wears five earrings in her right ear and four in her left.

On her back is a tattoo of a Celtic circle, displaying her pride in her Irish heritage. Sarah is different, and she loves it.

"I like individuality," said Sarah, a "B" student who'll attend Kansas City Kansas Community College after graduation from Washington High. "I'm making myself a better person.

"I just think I'm perfecting myself, and I like that kind of thing. I am always trying to make myself better.

"I'm also opening other people up to what they could do, too."

Sarah is part of the diverse student body at Washington High. The teens are black, white, Hispanic, American Indian and Asian-American.

But they're also different in their styles, abilities, dress, ambitions, dreams and expression.

"I think if everybody was different in their own way and showed it they would all be perfecting themselves and letting themselves shine through," Sarah said. "I think it's cool to put a little spice in things—something that's different that people don't expect you to do."

Her friend, Tamra D. Zemaitis, 18, who graduated from Washington High in May, embraces Sarah's uniqueness.

"She's my best friend," said Tamra, who shares Sarah's flare. "She's a very brave, outrageous, courageous person. I love her sense of style."

Some people don't. "Oh, some people freak out," Sarah said.

Their jaws drop. They point and stare. Some say awful things. But the majority likes her individuality and willingness to express it.

Many wish they had the courage to do such things when they were young. Sarah's mother, Joyce Enright, is one of her supporters. She said Sarah is a good daughter, makes good grades, doesn't do drugs or run the streets.

"I think it's kind of pretty," Enright said. "I don't think a whole lot of people could pull it off like she does. I don't always approve of it, but it's not the end of the world."

But reality sometimes causes Sarah to morph back to normal. She knows she gets hired for jobs more quickly when she looks like "the girl next door."

Years from now, no one looking at *The Hatchet* would ever know the real Sarah unless they knew her way back when—at Washington High School.

PORTRAIT:
LaTisha and Latoya Castleberry

An assertive beginning on adult life

LaTisha and Latoya Castleberry got a head start on their dreams last school year at Washington High School.

I got to know the twins during the first couple of years of my studies with the Class of 1999. I met LaTisha when she was a freshman in Alice Bennett's English class and Latoya when she was a sophomore in Beatrice McKindra's English class.

I've sat with them and their classmates since their freshman year. I plan to remain with the class until graduation in the spring. But Latoya and LaTisha don't.

The 17-year-olds graduated a year early along with Kevin Bilberry and Jonathan Finley, whom I also met when they were freshmen in Bennett's English class. I found out about their ambitious move when I picked up my copy of the 1997-98 Washington High School yearbook.

Being in a rush to embark on adult adventures is a hallmark of youth.

The twins said they went to night school and summer school while working two jobs each so they could get a jump on achieving their dreams. When their friends were beginning their senior year, LaTisha and Latoya were starting as freshmen at Kansas City Kansas Community College.

Each twin has goals. LaTisha is studying to be a nurse. Eventually she wants to become an obstetrician and gynecologist.

Latoya is studying to be a paralegal. In 10 years, she wants to be a homeowner, and in 20 years she plans to be a corporate lawyer.

LaTisha said some of their friends were disappointed that their classroom connection dating to grade school was being severed. But the twins said they couldn't afford to wait to graduate in 1999.

"We figured it was the best thing to do other than drop out," LaTisha said. "What did it take?

"A lot of hard work and dedication."

Each tirelessly tackled the task. Their inspiration has a heartbeat—Latoya's 17-month-old daughter, Jada.

"She's like my motivation," Latoya said.

LaTisha helped the doctor deliver Jada on May 29, 1997. It's given her an undying desire to serve the health-care needs of children and women.

"As far as my career, it's looking up," LaTisha said. "I'm really confident about it."

But it took some time for the twins to arrive at that conclusion. Things had not always gone smoothly.

LaTisha remembered the problems with her sister's pregnancy. "When she suffered, I suffered," LaTisha said.

That deep, extrasensory tie comes from being twins. "It was hard being there for her and myself," LaTisha said.

They have a younger sister, Tephanie, 16, and a brother, Joseph, 15, at Washington High, who also needed their support. But through hard work, the family has prevailed.

"I feel anybody can do anything if they try hard enough," LaTisha said.

The twins credit their grandparents, Ellis and Carole Castleberry, with whom they live, for their strong work ethic.

"I'm so proud of them," Carole Castleberry said. "They have worked so hard."

Each twin counts the other as her biggest fan and role model. "The future looks pretty bright," LaTisha said.

The twins plan to stay in touch with their friends even though the twins have advanced to the independent adult life of college. They'll even be at the graduation, too, in the audience with me applauding the Class of 1999 at Washington High.

PORTRAIT:
Jeanine Hegwood

Helping her reach a field of dreams

Jeanine Hegwood and I passed notes back and forth recently in Dennis Bobbitt's American government class.

I hadn't done that in nearly 30 years. The seemingly juvenile act occurred as Bobbitt talked about important stuff—the Constitution, tests, voting ... .

But the note Jeanine and I exchanged was important, too. It began with her question before the 7:25 a.m. bell: "Mr. Diuguid, will you write a letter of recommendation for me? It's for a college scholarship."

I couldn't say no. Others apparently hadn't either.

I was among hundreds of people last week who cheered for Jeanine at the Black Achiever's dinner. She and her classmates, Tim Adams, Jason Randall, Andrea Smith, Khaliah Sykes and Natalie Washington, were among the 21 high school scholarship recipients.

They made Washington High School the top scholarship winner at the event, honoring the Rev. Martin Luther King Jr.'s birthday. I told them and their parents how proud I was, too.

Jeanine, however, was seeking my help for a different scholarship. She, Tim, Jason, Andrea, Khaliah and Natalie are among the many seniors I've gotten to know since 1995.

Jeanine is sharp. I've seen her cut through confusion in class discussions to expose the heart of a lesson. She's also pragmatic, engaging, principled and motivated. She cares about her future, her class and her school. I've seen her perform at basketball games, playing the clarinet in the band.

She's also kept me honest. In 1996-97 Jeanine questioned my motives and my note-taking in her sophomore English class.

In 1997-98, she called me at home. Though shaken, she was the first to tell me her longtime schoolmate and friend, Justin Stanley, had been shot

130

to death.

Getting to know good students like Jeanine puts me in the enviable position of being able to help them with letters of recommendation or references. It's not a new thing for me.

In 1995-96 Washington High freshman Alex Chapman asked me for a job reference. I often do the same thing for students whom I'd taught in the annual Kansas City Association of Black Journalists Minority Student Journalism Workshop.

Jeanine just tapped a new source at her disposal. I asked her to whom I needed to send the letter.

She wrote it on a piece of her notebook paper with a Jan. 15 deadline and passed it to me in class. Jeanine also instructed me to say in the letter who I was, how long I'd known her and to comment on her character.

That provoked me to write other questions on her paper and pass it back to her. We'd had these conversations before. She just jarred my memory.

Jeanine has a 3.7 grade point average and is president of the National Honor Society, flag team captain, and a member of the marching band, DECA, Key Club, student council, gospel choir and Fellowship of Christian Athletes. Jeanine runs track and cross country. Her community service includes involvement in Kansas City Promise. After graduating in May she plans to attend Kansas State University to study sports medicine. Her hope is to become an athletic trainer for the Women's National Basketball Association.

I hope the Jan. 4 letter I wrote helps her get to where she wants to go.

PORTRAIT:
William Hawkins

Student's deeds speak volumes

It takes extra effort to avoid overlooking the students who get drowned out by the noise of everything else at Washington High School.

William Hawkins has been among the more reserved seniors, but he's kept me doing double takes since I began studying with students in the Class of 1999.

William and I have always exchanged greetings.

But he'd have been one of the easiest students to misread because he's among the quietest. Over the years, however, he has continually surprised me.

About three years ago, I learned he was on the tennis team after I quizzed him about a tennis racket he was carrying at an after-school event.

I attended a wrestling tournament last year and told William when I saw him suited up that I didn't know he was on the team. I also didn't know he played football during his freshman and junior years.

I was clueless about his playing the violin in the school orchestra and chamber groups. William, 17, has played since he was 3 and is involved in the Kansas City Youth Symphony.

He also surprised me one morning as we walked to the school library, saying he planned to attend Kansas State University and become a physician.

William added recently that his goal is to become a surgeon.

He has the grades to do it. He has a 3.78 grade-point average, is a member of the National Honor Society, and he's always earned A's in his favorite subjects—math and science.

"Numbers are easy for me," William said.

I told him he almost didn't register on my radar screen because he's so quiet in school.

"I'm not sure that I am," William responded. "Most of the time I'm paying attention to what the teachers have to say and not talking."

I watched William drown out a noisy gymnasium and listen intently to Brook Penca, his wrestling coach. Penca barked encouragement as William competed in the 135-pound weight class at the recent Bulldog Invitational K.C. Wyandotte Wrestling Tournament.

The hard-fought match against a tough Topeka opponent lasted about nine minutes. William won with a pin.

"He's probably our most improved wrestler who has an opportunity to possibly get to state this year, and that's what we're hoping for," Penca said.

"William is one of those young men who never says a cross word," Penca said. "He comes and works very hard.

"Through his perseverance he's starting to get the desired results that he wants. He's a thinker. He thinks about things, not just in wrestling but in life."

William's dad, Franklin A. Hawkins, agreed. Perseverance, honesty and integrity are William's greatest attributes. "No matter what he sets his mind to he's going to figure out how to do it," Hawkins said.

William said his goal is to become a better person by helping people and pursuing things that are mentally, physically and emotionally challenging. He quietly drives himself to maximize his strengths and minimize his mistakes.

"I'm just persistent basically in practicing and studying," William said. "All the hard work will pay off later."

That kind of quiet confidence, persistence and performance will speak loudly for William in college and long after he leaves Washington High School.

PORTRAIT:
Khaliah Sykes

Giving back to their community

Khaliah Sykes gave me her business card outside of Washington High School.

I never had personalized business cards when I was her age. But I also wasn't as involved as this 17-year-old senior is.

I'd met Khaliah recently at Kennedy Elementary School, where she tutors Pat Bush's fifth-graders. It's part of the community service Khaliah does for credit in Dennis Bobbitt's American government class at Washington High.

She also coordinates the program, connecting about 10 of her classmates with community needs. It started in October. In November the seniors volunteered at the polls to help children cast mock ballots in Kids Voting—Wyandotte County.

Now the seniors are volunteering in schools. At Kennedy Elementary, Khaliah and I peeked in on Tierra Hall, who had second-graders mesmerized as she read them "Snow White and the Seven Dwarfs."

It's been cool to watch this grown-up quality develop in the Class of 1999.

The community is reaching out to the seniors more than ever before. Many of the seniors are extending an eager helping hand back.

The students are feeling the real-world grip of many needs, the clinging weight of responsibility and the unkind consequences of inaction. The community rejoices in the youthful tonic of commitment from high-achieving students such as Khaliah.

"It's all about caring and helping individuals and not working against them," said Khaliah, who has a 3.75 grade point average, is in the National Honor Society and plans to be a lawyer. "In so many ways we're helping the community. The students are part of the community."

Bush gave her fifth-graders about a dozen division problems to solve.

Khaliah, who works part-time as a teller at Security Bank in Kansas City, Kan., helped Marvelle Stubbs, 11, divide 7 into 682.

"I think it's nice that she helps," Marvelle said, beaming, after solving the problem.

"The kids really seem to accept her because she's closer to their age," Bush said. Positive role models reinforcing the value of a good education are essential.

"School? Basically it's your foundation for what you can achieve in life," Khaliah said as she helped Chenika Bray, 10.

"If they can have someone older come in and say, 'This is important; this is normal,' then things are going to be OK," said Bush, who knew Khaliah when she was a pupil at Douglass Elementary School. "It's like a non-threatening situation for both of them."

Khaliah, who will be in the Delta Sigma Theta Cotillion on April 3 at the Hyatt Regency Crown Center hotel, said she enjoys helping and learning what it's like to be a kid again.

"There is just one teacher, and one teacher can't get around to every student," Khaliah said. "It's just a chance to give back to the community."

Bobbitt said community service is a natural part of his American government class.

"If you want your community to be strong, you have to go back and build that community," he said. "I want this community to get strong. One of the ways that is going to happen is to start with the kids."

The match is perfect for the students and the community of Washington High School.

Part IV
Chapter 5
Sports: An Unnecessary Distraction?

Schools use many Trojan Horses to get students to take an interest in education. Sports is among the biggest.

C all me a purist when it comes to education. The essentials include teachers, administrators, support personnel, books, notepaper, pencils, pens, computers and community involvement. But a constant interloper in the learning process is athletics. In school, it starts with mandatory gym classes, which many students love to hate. Then it graduates to organized school district supported team sports, enlisting the best athletes as players. Even many of the recalcitrant gym class members become religious fans of a school's many teams as sports and those who play take on an aura of demigods on school campuses. Academics often get lost in this cheering community of prestige and money in sports. High school sports serve as a training and proving ground with the best graduating later to college competition and the true champions advancing to professional leagues afterward. But the four years in high school and at least four years in college is such a fleeting period. If it's squandered on athletics at the expense of academics, it's nearly impossible to recoup. For many young males fixated on their favorite televised games, sports seems to be the only means to realize their dreams of notoriety, influence and fame. Excelling in school gets left behind. I found that trend among some students at Washington High School, where too many of the young men often seemed to be off on another track. Their attention was diverted from their studies by the media, which made sports and other things seem more alluring and important. The following column, **"Media fluff danger is a no-brainer,"** offers that insight.

A troubling trend came into focus at my oldest daughter's recent induction into the National Junior Honor Society.

Adrianne, 13, was among 90 students at her middle school who earned membership into the meritorious group. But as the honorees went on stage, I wondered out loud: "Where are the boys?"

The girls outnumbered the boys by a 2-1 ratio. It was radically different from my school days when the boys took most of the awards and the bows.

I thought what I witnessed was a fluke, but it happened again at a community scholarship ceremony I attended, where nine awards went to females and two went to males.

It occurred again at a suburban high school, where I gave out a scholar-athlete award from *The Kansas City Star*. In past years, I've given it to guys. This year it went to a young woman.

In fact, 51 of *The Star*'s 84 scholar-athlete awards for 1997 went to young women. Most of the other scholarships and honors handed out at the school that night went to young women.

At a second suburban high school, I handed out two Black Achievers Society scholarships—both to young women. But I also noted that 57 awards went to young men while 101 went to young women.

It's great that young women are high achievers. But the question still remains: "Where are the guys?"

Adrianne said getting "A" grades didn't seem to be a guy thing. They're hooked on sports.

But many are more armchair athletes than players. Guys talk sports and channel surf the changing sports seasons for games on television.

The media also market sports, action adventure movies, video games and TV shows to males. Savvy corporations feed guys a steady media junk food diet, and a lot of males drag many females to that trough.

On the other hand, a lot of that mental junk food doesn't

appeal to females, so they channel their energy elsewhere. In addition, Take Our Daughters to Work Day and other efforts to boost young women's academic prowess and self-esteem have driven them to focus on their long-term future instead of short-term entertainment.

According to recent reports, this trend is continuing. In an article titled, "Girls winning brain game," Alaina Sue Potrikus writes that "three out of five members of high school National Honor Societies today are girls. Girls outnumber boys 124 to 100 in advanced placement courses. As recently as 1987, boys outnumbered girls in those demanding classes." Potrikus goes on to point out that "[a] survey of U.S. high school seniors who took the SAT in 2000 found that 44 percent of the young women reported A averages. Among men, 35 percent did. And a count of valedictorians in the Philadelphia area last spring turned up 106 females and only 64 males."

It's as if the gender battle has shifted to a conflict of impulse vs. intellect. More males seem to impulsively follow their appetites to gorge on commercial fluff. But more females to whom the media messages aren't primarily aimed seem to stay intellectually trained on scholastics.

The short-term pleasures of sports became a hot topic during a talk I gave on journalism at a suburban high school in 1996. As I wrote in a column headlined, **"Sports can become a petty goal,"**

> Everything went well until one student asked whether I liked sports.
>
> I had just finished telling the students to take their studies seriously, no matter how silly or worthless the work might seem. Eventually, they'll need every scrap of information, from kindergarten—where kids first learn how to get along with others—through college.
>
> Each class offers a smorgasbord of knowledge. Young people need to block out distractions and eat like there's no tomorrow at such brain-food buffets to succeed in school and in future careers.

I explained that students must maintain high levels of curiosity and have voracious appetites for information because technological changes will force them to continue learning long after they leave school.

The consequences of being a slacker are grim. Unemployment lines stretch long with people who've failed to be high achievers. Then I got hit with the question about sports.

I am not a fan, and I don't speak sports.

I confessed those shortcomings to the class. Then I explained that sports is a form of entertainment, one that diverts their attention from studies and jobs. I also asked the inquiring student whether having fun was his only goal in life.

His answer was simple: "Yes."

That helped me understand why many preteen and adolescent boys whom I've quizzed on what they want to be when they grow up frown on school but bank on careers in basketball, football or baseball. They've been dazzled by powerful media images of star athletes having "fun" playing games.

But most boys have about as much of a chance of becoming pro ballplayers making millions of dollars as I do of winning the lottery—and I don't gamble.

I also realized why many preteen and adolescent girls whom I've quizzed about school and careers have solid, attainable objectives. In a backward way they've benefited from the longstanding gender bias in the media and in sports.

They don't have soufflé heroes diverting their attention from day-to-day studies and real-world goals. I thanked the boy for asking the question and then told the class that life has to be about more than fun.

Games and sports often tumble together, siphoning

139

money and time from fans like a clothes dryer evaporates moisture. When taken in moderation, that's OK.

But I told the students that they and others would be enriched if they gave their time, attention and resources to community causes. It's better for them to start giving back to society when they're young than to get into an early life-long habit of "taking" and gorging themselves on the world's resources solely for fun and pleasure.

I told the young people to also read to expand their critical thinking and analytical skills. People who follow impulses and go with gut feelings are easily swayed by emotion.

Those who study can pose serious, thoughtful questions. They can see through scams and overcome challenges.

One last thing: Young people are the world's greatest consumers.

They can either spend their time, attention and resources on mindless junk food such as sports, or they can fill up on education at schools—the all-you-can-eat buffets of knowledge and ideas.

Students, however, see things differently. Steve Brown made that clear to me when he came over to my student desk to talk to me about the above column. That's just not the way it is, he said. For them, sports keeps them interested in school. It brings them back to class each school day especially when they're bored with learning. Participating in sports compels them to continue to study so they can continue to play and so their grades won't turn talent scouts' attention to other aspiring athletes. Sports for many of them is the end-all of education.

Constant exposure to the students helped to soften my hard edge against the diverting influence sports has on education. In the best situation, sports teaches young people how to be competitive, how to win with humility and to lose while gaining lessons in perseverance and dignity. Sports is an entry point, or another window through which educators get students to invest their time and attention in school. It's a way to reach young people when all else fails, a way for coaches in the many sports, who also are teachers, to function as some of the best advocates for education. That keeps kids and schools in the game of serving our community and this country. Following the students to their extracurricular practices and games also served to give me that new insight from the skyscraper called education.

The fact that females are apparently expending more intellectual effort than males doesn't mean, of course, that young women aren't engaged in and enthusiastic about sports. Many of the girls at Washington High School were members of the school's sports teams. One of the oddest things I encountered at Washington High School was trying to ensure that I gave the young men and young women equal time. In contrast to my school days, the young women now seemed more involved and eager to share. Seeing the girls play basketball was just as cool as watching the boys' game. A column headlined, **"This game is a real sign of progress,"** brought that out.

Time ran out last school year before I could get to Keasha Cannon's and Mykie M. DeGraftenreed's special invitation at Washington High School.

Tiauda Taylor told me early this school year, so I could spend just as much time cheering for the girls as they played basketball for their school teams as I did for the boys a year ago.

I didn't know what to expect when I entered the gym and sat next to Scott Milkowart, who has let me study with the juniors in his three American history classes this year. I'd shot yearbook photos of boys' basketball for my high school in 1972-73.

Girls' basketball like this didn't exist at my old school. Milkowart said a lot had changed. The Washington vs. Bishop Ward game last month would be a treat.

"They can rock," Milkowart said of the Washington team.

141

The game was just as fast-paced and exciting as any I'd seen. The junior varsity Lady Cats played tough, smart basketball and won easily. Varsity followed with a decisive victory.

Milkowart was right. Keasha, a junior who suffered a knee injury and underwent surgery and physical therapy last school year, had a great game with steals, assists, terrific ball handling, layups and fabulous jump shots.

Juniors Mykie and Tiauda also played exceptionally well. Sara Hampton, a junior, smiled when I said I didn't know she was on the team.

I also didn't know that Tiauda was part of a basketball family. Her sisters Je T'aime Taylor, a senior, Tiffany Taylor, a sophomore, and Nellie Terry, a freshman, are all Lady Cats.

"I'm just so proud of them," said their mother, Carol Terry. "They're not on the street.

"They're not wanting to party. I think they see a different part of life."

The Lady Cats have the same hoop dreams that the male Wildcats at Washington High shared with me a year ago.

"I think I'll be playing it forever," said Mykie, 16, who makes A's and B's and appreciates the discipline from coach Wayne Lathrop.

She hopes to get a scholarship and play ball in college, where she plans to study to be an English teacher. She said being a leader on the court compels her to do well in academics.

Tiauda, 17, who makes A's and B's, hopes for a college basketball scholarship as part of her goals to become a model and fashion designer and to coach community basketball for girls.

Keasha, who averages 17 to 18 points a game, is on the

honor roll. She's shooting for college scholarships and a degree in physical therapy, computer science or accounting.

"I'd love to play in the Women's National Basketball Association," said Keasha, 17. "It's a new challenge for me."

She's not as interested in women's pro sports salaries, which are bounding up to men's, as much as she wants to be on a team.

"It doesn't matter how much they'd pay me," Keasha said. "I'd just play for the fun of it."

The Lady Cats added that they're encouraged that their high school is paying more attention to girls' sports. Cheerleaders and more people are showing up for their games, Tiauda and Mykie said.

School officials sometimes have to be reminded to make programs and announce when the girls have won.

But that's OK, Keasha said. "The harder they are on us the better it will make us in life," she said.

That's a winning attitude that I wish everyone had.

By showing me that sports could be a valuable and motivating part of their school activities, and that school didn't have to be all academic all of the time, the girls at Washington High School taught me how to be a better parent to my own daughters in their athletic pursuits. In essence these are all our kids. For me, that has come to mean that their participation in sports counts, especially when that participation doesn't become the sole focus but complements and enhances the students' intellectual effort. We have to applaud our young people—no matter what their greatest talents and achievements are—and value them because none of them will be kids forever. That came out in a column headlined, **"Parents: Fill those bleachers."**

It had to happen.

On Friday I went to Independence to watch my 14-year-old daughter, Adrianne, compete in her first high school swim meet. I like the fact that it was Independence. It signified a time of strength, self-reliance and growing up, and I had to cheer her on.

But in the steamy Henley Aquatic Center, I also found veteran swimmers I've been studying with at Washington High School.

I'd met Sarah Finney, Corey Brinton and Sara Hampton when they were freshmen in 1995 in Alice Bennett's English classes. I cheered for them in April at a swim meet they'd invited me to attend.

I told them I didn't know they'd be among the swimmers from 20 high schools area wide and as far away as Warrensburg, Mo., competing in the relays. I said it was an added benefit in being there to watch Adrianne.

But Julie Brinton, Corey's mom, joked, "Well, who are you going to cheer for now?"

I laughed and said I was applauding for every teen I knew at the pool. I yelled praise to Adrianne and her teammates, and gave high-fives Friday to Sara, Corey and Sarah when they climbed into the aquatic center bleachers to celebrate their success with Julie Brinton and me.

But I also got to praise swimmers from Hickman Mills and Lee's Summit, who reminded me that we'd met years ago when I'd spoken to their classes. I was impressed that they remembered, and I was impressed that they, too, were swimmers.

I had just seen Corey on Thursday, when students had finished tests on the Civil War and moved into the Reconstruction. The late 1800s were a national time of rebuilding after slavery and the war, just as the late 1900s have been an era of new hope and equality for girls and women in sports and in life.

I've seen Bennett, Beatrice McKindra and Scott Milko-

wart devote just as much attention to helping the girls succeed in class as the boys. Girls' swim coaches Nancy
Browne and Jennifer Anderson add to that effort.

The support of parents is an essential element, Julie
Brinton said. She was among several Washington High
School parents riding the hard, backaching bleachers out of
love and support for their daughters.

"It makes a big difference when parents come to support us," Corey said after I told her that Adrianne hadn't
expected me to be there.

When the girls went back to swim, I told Julie Brinton
that knowing so many kids created a major time-
management conflict for me. It meant choosing when to
cheer for Adrianne and her 11-year-old sister, Leslie, and
when to applaud the teens who've become a big part of my
life at Washington High School.

I've found that they're all our precious children, and ensuring their success must be every adult's prime directive.

Part IV
Chapter 6
Pushing for Higher Standards;
Raising Expectations Beyond
the "No Child Left Behind" Rhetoric

There are no acceptable losses in the ongoing struggle to educate America's children. Sadly, however, the losses seem to be growing.

PORTRAIT:
James R. Lindsey

Lessons in music and life

Crystal Barrientos stopped me in the hall earlier this school year to ask me to visit her music class at Washington High School. I couldn't say no.

I set a date with her teacher, James R. Lindsey, and stepped into a world filled with crescendos of discipline, hard work, pride, devotion and beautiful music. A passion for learning and performing filled the room.

It sparkled like the trophies gleaming in the sunlight by the wall of windows. The zeal also was as intoxicating as the will of the students to exceed their demanding teacher's expectations.

State competition starts this month. Making the cut is what the students have worked to achieve.

The class chanted Lindsey's motto: Good, better, best. Never let it rest until your good is your better and your better is your best.

I've seen that on many T-shirts that students have worn in the halls of Washington High School. I have heard students repeat the mantra in the years that I have shared with them.

Crystal's invitation took me to the source.

"It was so you could hear, so you could know what we're doing," Crystal said after class. "Mr. Lindsey is demanding on what we need to do to go to state competition.

"It's fun, but it's tiring. We work, and we work for the whole 1 1/2 hours."

The class took deep breaths and let the air out with a whoosh! that vibrated the room. The students ran through practice chords: hey, hey, hey, hey, hah, hah, hah, hah, hah, hah ... .

One-word wall posters add to the instruction: Posture, breathing, palate, vowels, diction, animation and focus on sound.

"You're breaking focus by doing anything other than what I want you to do," Lindsey emphasized to the class. "This is not fun. It's a rehearsal."

More warmups follow. "Mommy made me mash my M&Ms ... ," the students sing. The teens roll their shoulders and flex their neck muscles.

Shanell Morrow handed me a book of songs. "Shenandoah" was among the ones the students sang as a piano played.

Keenan Ramos sang a solo part for the teacher he admires.

"Mr. Lindsey is undoubtedly one of the best men I know," Keenan said. "He has taught me everything I know about singing.

"He's also taught me you can be a friend with a teacher, and you can have a good relationship with a teacher."

That doesn't mean Lindsey is a pushover. He stopped the chorus. "Do what whoever is standing here says!" Lindsey said.

"I've got to hear those basses," he added. "We've got no volume there."

Stanley Shannon said Lindsey enabled students to unhinge creatively.

"It's a class you can express yourself in," Stanley said.

Music in Lindsey's class is the channel through which Jennifer Rogers' emotions find a voice.

"I have some things I'm going through," she said. "That class is what helps me get through it."

Teachers like Lindsey who stress excellence find they have to meet the high demands of the students, too.

He told me after class he has to wear a lot of hats, including surrogate parent, confidant and friend because today's students, with many distractions at home and work, arrive at school with many needs.

"Never accept mediocrity," Lindsey tells them.

In a chorus, they sing that song back to him, and he responds to their many voices at Washington High School.

148

*I*n the United States today the population overall is being dumbed down. Public schools aim their teaching and achievement requirements mostly at the bulge of "average" children, and young people who are able to achieve above average often get lost in the system of education. The "average" standard at schools is reinforced by the mass media, which young people consume in vast quantities. Music, television, cable TV, video games and movies largely encourage people to not question, analyze or critically evaluate what they take in. Instead they push people to act on impulse, eliciting knee-jerk reactions that require little knowledge, thought, or understanding.

We must ask ourselves to what end this is taking place and who is benefiting from these trends. Stephanie G. Robinson, who in 1995 was principal partner with the Education Trust of the American Association for Higher Education, provided some answers, and I wrote about our conversation in a column headlined, **"When children graduate as thinkers, we all reap the rewards."** I met Robinson in the summer of 1995, before I became involved at Washington High School. Throughout the project, she served as one of my many advisers.

> Stephanie G. Robinson helped me understand why we need standards in education.

> I knew the standards movement would ensure that students graduate after proving on tests that they have knowledge as well as analytical and problem-solving skills. But Robinson opened my eyes when she explained why some people don't want that.

> Robinson recalled a conversation with an elected official in Washington who opposes the push for academic excellence. He asked: "If we raise the standards, who's going to mow my lawn?"

> That's vile, but many people want substandard education to ensure that the country has a large, low-wage, menial labor pool. To them, if everyone leaves school well-educated no one will want to mow lawns, be nannies, housekeepers, cooks or servants, or work for minimum wage.

149

Such thinking also may be behind the attack on affirmative action in education and California wanting to deny schooling to kids of illegal immigrants. But graduating poorly educated people will segregate them in chains to a generational cycle of poverty.

In reality, if students are elevated "to become thinkers, then the person who takes care of your kids takes care of them better and may be able to develop a business out of that," Robinson said.

"The person who mows your lawn maybe will be able to become a contributor to the economy by having a business rather than just working for somebody and increase the whole economic pie instead of having it finite," she said. "It's interesting to see how advances in technology have created some other jobs.

"But you've got to have people well-enough educated to be able to imagine new kinds of jobs. That's what efforts of this whole standards-based reform movement are all about. We can see that, where there are those things in place, kids do better."

The national push for education standards lost steam in 1994 with the Republican takeover in Congress, said Ruth Mitchell, Education Trust principal partner. But it has gained momentum in states like Missouri and Kansas.

Dale Dennis, interim education commissioner in Kansas, said elevated standards result in higher achievement and more economic development.

Orlo Shroyer, division of instruction assistant commissioner with the Missouri Department of Elementary and Secondary Education, said: "One of the major reasons for developing standards is we establish equity of opportunity across the state of Missouri for children."

It's needed because education has been on a 20-year slide in which students have graduated with eroded academic skills, Robinson said. They have multiple choice talents in a global marketplace that needs essay thinkers.

Right now many young people lack a deep and broad-based knowledge of mathematics, English, science and history. "It's the difference between thinking of history as a bunch of dates that are strung together but not of big trends and big ideas of how people live and work and exist together in groups," Robinson said.

Without critical thinking or analytical skills, workers won't question unethical or immoral tasks if profit is the motive. Consumers could be conned into buying useless things they can't afford, and the nation would be vulnerable to wholesale manipulation.

Politicians on TV could sway public opinion in a heartbeat by superimposing their views on people who react to emotion rather than reading to search for more facts and analysis. Raising standards in education may be our only salvation from those who would profit by ensuring that the movement dies and goes away.

Before I started writing about Washington High School, I encountered students who were victims of the dumbing down problem that Robinson described. This incident, however, occurred in the Kansas City School District at one of its best schools. I wrote about it in a column that ran under the headline **"Simple isn't the answer."** I'd been invited to work with a ninth-grade literature and composition class. I'd asked the students to think and write four sentences in five minutes on anything they had seen or experienced that morning. Afterward they had to read their work out loud and help evaluate the essays they heard. But when I pressed them with questions and gave them my input, trying to show them that they needed to think before putting pen to paper and to learn that they need to write well now to get good jobs in the future, the students rebelled. The trigger was my saying that

one student's work "connoted" more than what was written. "What does 'connoted' mean?" a 14-year-old boy asked.

I could have told him, but instead I asked him to look it up. A girl handed him a dictionary. I spelled the word be-

151

cause he didn't know where to start and had him read the definition to the class.

He still didn't get it so I defined it in the context of the sentence. Then he asked, "Who are you trying to impress?"

He accused me of using big words that the class couldn't understand. Other students chimed in to the unruly chorus saying I was negative, and one girl asked, "Why can't you talk to us on our level?"

How curious, I thought. They wanted me to treat them like adults but speak to them as if they would always be kids.

I rebutted their charges and said I was just pushing them to prepare them for what they'll encounter in the future, because they won't be teens forever.

I said I could have used "Dick and Jane" sentences, but that wouldn't stretch them to a higher level of thought. That made them angrier and louder. The bell finally ended the argument.

The teachers apologized to me afterward, but they didn't know what had provoked the outrage. It was the polite thing to do but it shows that some teachers are perhaps not pressing students to perform and meet higher standards. Even though this was one incident, other such situations occur too frequently to be overlooked.

A similar type of tension surfaced in Beatrice McKindra's sophomore class at Washington High School more than a year later. Her students became animated and agitated when they realized that their persistent word-use and spelling errors on essays and exams were unacceptable. In a column headlined, **"Employers will shun students who shunned writing lessons,"**

McKindra's kids explained that they'd fallen into a habit of writing as they talked or in mimicking in ink what they heard among their peers, at home, on television and radio, and in videos.

One teen said she regularly wrote "4" instead of "for."

Another student said he was accustomed to writing "alright" and never "all right."

"It's always two words," McKindra said.

He responded: "I didn't know that!"

Other students were confounded by "to," "two" and "too." Some were bummed on "all together" and "altogether"; "who's" and "whose"; "affect" and "effect"; and "their," "they're" and "there." In another class McKindra explained when to use "lay," "lie" and "lain."

"That don't sound right," a student blurted out.

Then McKindra identified what she saw as one of the students' biggest problems: "You're practicing those incorrect usages informally, and when you get to formal writing, you forget. I want to bring this up in your minds."

The different standards of usage these students have to confront is a source of great confusion for many of them, as I found out during an incident that took place in Alice Bennett's classroom and that I wrote about in a column headlined, **"These days, making the grade in school means smart timing."** That day, the students were going to take a test, and before the test started, one of them came to sit by me and

pushed a dollar bill from his desktop to mine.

"Mr. Diuguid, will you take this test for me?" he asked only half-jokingly. "I'll give you a dollar."

I was being hustled by a pretty good hustler. But I returned the teen's dollar and told him he'd have to solo on the vocabulary portion of the standardized achievement test. "You can do a lot better than I can," I said.

When the test started, every hallway noise and student

sigh echoed throughout the classroom. The teen with the dollar initially filled the silence with whispers. "Mr. Diuguid, what's a client?" he asked, seeking help on his test.

He read the options aloud. I told him to think and then pick the one he thought was correct.

He did and then whispered again. "Mr. Diuguid! What's an ordeal?"

I just looked at him.

"I'll just put confusion," he said of his multiple choice options, "because I'm confused."

Students often deal with their quandaries by becoming angry, because they see their abilities falling short of an outsider's expectations. That isn't good because life is about expectations—those being set and met. Robinson said:

Any kid who is confronted with something that they don't want to see, the first reaction is anger and kill the messenger. We're reaping the consequences of 20 years or more in which the quality of instruction and the expectations were low both in what was expected to be learned and what was taught to a large segment of the population.

She referred to it as "education malpractice." Teachers face the heat from students who don't understand why they have to stretch their minds, from parents who complain when their kids get bad grades, and from administrators who offer little or no support. Teachers then feel outnumbered, and some surrender and dumb down their lessons just to survive another year.

But these four major players in the education operating room aren't entirely to blame for the "malpractice" they perpetuate. The media have a hand in it as well. Keep this in mind: the hell we're creating in not educating and making lifelong learners out of students is a journalist's paradise because those kids whom the system deems "acceptable losses" in the war on learning will end up making major headlines in the media. So here is the Catch-22 situation. This is the problem that Robinson described. Too many parents and other adults kill their kids' curiosity by not responding to them and their questions. How often have you heard a parent tell a child, "Shut up, and leave me alone!" or "Please don't ask me those stupid questions!" Then they give these children to the media by parking them in front of the television, and the media take care of them with violence, racism, sexism, insecurities and a heavy dependence on buying more things for a happiness they can never own. As Cornell West put it in a speech given on June 25, 2003, at the Lannan Foundation in Santa Fe, New Mexico, Americans have an "anti-intellectual culture. Why, in part? It's a business civilization; it's a market-driven civilization, what Henry James called a hotel civilization. Obsessed with comfort, convenience, contentment. Not wanting to engage in Socratic activity that unsettles and unnerves and un-houses people." David Walsh deals with it in his book *Selling Out America's Children: How America Puts Profits Before Values – and What Parents Can Do.* That sellout goes on right into the prisons and right into the graves for our children. Then journalists get to document the disaster that all the people in the media have helped create.

Television is the most heavily consumed and influential branch of the media and is a major part of the problem. In a critical assessment of the industry, "The State of the News Media 2004" study said that 83 percent of Americans get most of their news from television. That's not good in our democracy, which depends on people of all ages being more informed than television reporting will allow. In a column headlined **"Teen generation's thoughts developed with TV messages,"** I expressed concern about

> the media bath students daily take and how it affects them.
>
> That surfaced in an earlier discussion I had with the students. I sought their input on how welfare should be reformed and poverty eliminated for a speech I had to give at a recent Reform Organization of Welfare conference. This predated the harshness that Welfare Reform wrought under

the Clinton administration.

The students were eager to help. Adrian Hutson thought our country should stop aiding other nations.

Terry Wheat agreed, saying: "We should help ourselves before going to help other people. If we are in debt, why should we go fight for other people when the money should be used for a better cause?"

Corey Brinton and Steve Brown said teen moms shouldn't get more welfare if they have a second child. "That would eliminate teenage pregnancy," Corey said.

"They should know they can't take care of the babies themselves," Steve said.

The criminal justice system should be stricter, Damon Culter said. "If you do the crime you ought to do the time, no matter what," he said.

A couple of anomalies surfaced. Patrick George said jobs should pay more and college should be free to give youths more opportunities. Others disagreed.

Damon also said health-care costs should be lowered. "People wouldn't have to worry about paying all their money out to keep their families healthy," he said.

But other voices drowned him out. I told the people at the welfare reform conference that the students seemed like 1950s kids growing up in the high-tech '90s.

That's partly because they're kids of the communications age, in which TV is the dominant voice teaching and guiding their development. They were born when Ronald Reagan was president and grew up listening to conservative-speak from George Bush, Bob Dole, Newt Gingrich and waffling moderates like President Bill Clinton.

They're simply giving back what they've gotten as plugged-in, dumbed-down, TV-addicted—yet conservative—kids of our times.

When I wrote the column entitled, **"Masked in stereotypes, television loses sight of self-esteem"** (see Chapter 3), in which I had attacked some of the students' favorite shows for being garbage filled with stereotypes of African Americans, students felt compelled to let me know that television to them was just entertainment and nothing more. I wrote about the vehemence of one group of teens in support of their TV shows in a column headlined, **"Attacked from all sides."** I had been asked to speak to students at Ruskin High School about media stereotypes, making me the match that ignited an explosive discussion. I mentioned that, in the sitcoms featuring African Americans,

> Black men are pictured as Stepin Fetchit, shucking-and-jiving, skirt-chasing, eye-rolling buffoons. Black women play the straight role to them or they're materialistic, belligerent characters with major attitudes.

> I gave that spiel to about 50 students in the Ruskin Media Center, and then they gave it back with animation and outrage: How dare I attack the beloved electronic marvel they've worshiped all of their lives.

> I provoked them, and many responded, treating me like "Ricki Lake" TV talk show trash. De'Shonna Wade wrote about the encounter in the latest issue of the school paper, *the Ruskin Hi-Light.*

> First the students accused me of trashing the only shows featuring African Americans on television.

> I responded, saying sitcoms offer only a narrow view of black people in America. Sure, black people are funny. But no one group is that funny.

> Where are the dramas and the mysteries, and I'm not talking about "Cops" or "America's Most Wanted." The media fail to give the world a complete picture of African Americans, which is why many people of all colors define blacks by the stereotypes they see on TV.

> But the students didn't buy my logic. Instead, they accused me of being a sell-out and an Uncle Tom for attack-

ing the few black shows on TV. After all, it's only entertainment, they said.

No, it's poison. The negative images that people get
from the media in our segregated society confront African
Americans constantly. Blacks get it in school, where they
are thought to have little intellect, and they get it at work,
where they must compete for jobs, promotions and pay
raises with others who don't wear racism's chains.

The students cried that they were helpless to change the
media so they accept it, warts and all. I said that through
phone calls and letters they could have a voice in creating
better media images of people of color and women for everyone.

Then the class shifted again and blasted me for being
too Afrocentric and for not taking into consideration the
white students in the mostly black audience. Now that's a
first.

I'd given this talk at universities, community colleges,
and elementary, middle and high schools in Missouri and
Kansas. But I'd never been slammed for being an Uncle
Tom, a sell-out and Afrocentric in the same hour by the
same class.

I shook that punch and gave one of my own. I told the
students that all of our lives, we and our ancestors had
learned Eurocentric lessons in history, sociology, language, psychology, culture, science, art, music, sports and
more.

What's wrong with exposing everyone in the room to
new thoughts and Afrocentric lessons, especially when it's
about tearing down stereotypes and replacing them with
the truth?

It is obvious from the exchange described above that the students found it easier to swallow the stereotypes presented on TV
than to recognize the danger and call for the truth. They have sur-
rendered to the relentless onslaught of media images they are ex-

posed to every day. But it isn't just TV that has captured the minds of today's students. Other forms of media have been just as enslaving. In the years I followed the Class of 1999 at Washington High in Kansas City, Kan., I learned just how hooked many teenagers are on media hype. I continued to beat the drum against mindless overconsumption of the media in a column headlined **"Media hype casts a spell over youths."** I noted that

Adults put the sweet, seductive poison in kids' faces and then wonder what's wrong with kids.

Young people are bombarded with scads of media messages from cold corporations and dead rappers like no previous generation. They're eating it up, and it's consuming them.

Colorful Coke machines hum in the school's corridors, and students stop for a drink between classes. Expensive starter jackets, shirts, pants and athletic shoes fill the halls.

Students and parents pay hundreds of dollars for the clothes that advertise companies and sports teams. I always thought corporations should pay people to burden their bodies with commercial hype.

Schoolwork takes a back seat to the hype.

"I think we have spoiled them," Beatrice McKindra said. "They are more audiovisual.

"They watch a lot of television. They would rather watch than read and think. We have spoon-fed them. I, too, am guilty."

The students sometimes act out what they see on TV. A pep rally I attended last school year was like a music video, louder and more aggressive than the tame things in my school days.

Then there was a basketball game I went to this year. It was like those when I was in high school, except for the tattoos that marked some players' bodies.

159

TV sports stars tattoo their flesh. Why shouldn't teens?

At the end of the game, people began to leave the bleachers, until a man with a sack started tossing palm-sized orange balls into the stands. Students tumbled madly over others to get them.

One girl held up her prize. On the ball were the words "Just for Feet," a popular Kansas City area athletic shoe store and another media message.

In fact, in his book *Corporateering*, published in 2003, Jamie Court wrote that "advertising money directed at children has grown twenty-fold during the last ten years. Corporations spend $12 billion per year marketing to children . . . . The child's consciousness has been put up for sale in schools, in the home, and in the community" (104). In addition to the soft drinks sold in the corridors, Channel One, "a commercial television broadcast that includes advertising," is shown in the classrooms of "one-quarter of all middle schools," according to a September 2000 report done by the General Accounting Office (105). I experienced Channel One first hand in Alice Bennett's classroom, and described the event in the column previously cited, and headlined **"Teen generation's thoughts developed with TV messages."**

Channel One News played on a color TV bolted to the wall in Room 43 for the plugged-in and turned-on students of the 1990s.

It was the first time I'd seen the news and current events program since schools nationwide started using it in March 1990. The show is controversial because it hits captive teen audiences with commercials, which pay for the news.

The first Channel One News story was on terrorist bombings in Israel, which threaten Middle East peace efforts. A pizza ad followed.

A chewing gum ad came next and then a news story on smokeless tobacco. Teenage boys spit for the cameras. The class winced.

Boys on the show liked to chew. Girls said it's gross, and smokeless tobacco gives boys bad breath.

The camera showed the damage to gums and teeth from chewing. Smokeless tobacco also makes people more prone to strokes, heart disease and cancers, a young TV reporter said.

An athletic shoe commercial followed, and then an acne cream ad. The chewing tobacco story returned briefly, and then the two-story, four-commercial TV newscast ended.

A class discussion followed, focusing on shredded bubble gum that comes in a tobacco-like pouch, which could direct kids to smokeless tobacco. "It appears to be harmless," Alice Bennett said.

"After all, it's just bubble gum, isn't it?" she said. "But it's such an imitation!"

Two stories lost among twice as many commercials in less than one class period—what is Channel One really teaching our children? As Court writes, they "have been taught the logic of the invisible hand—that everything is for sale, corporations are your friend, and things can be valued more than people" (104). Furthermore, says Court,

Academic researchers from across the nation contend that this change of social custom has contributed to significant physical and psychological problems among youth. These are among the broad societal consequences associated with the corporate capture of the consciousness of impressionable children who, unlike adults, are often unable to distinguish truth from fiction (104).

Or smokeless tobacco from bubble gum?

The young man in Bennett's class who offered me a dollar to take his test for him had certainly bought the idea that "everything is for sale." That is distressing in and of itself. But another of the worrisome "problems among youth" that surfaced during my years at Washington High School was what I pointed out earlier: that "schoolwork takes a back seat to hype." Many teens showed me that they're "A" students on TV shows but that they struggle with their studies. They often arrive in class without the basics—pens, pencils, books and papers. Like the student who tried to bribe me to take his exam for him, many "do not take standardized tests seriously," commented Alice Bennett. "Why should they," she continued. "They see no consequence, and there's no encouragement at home."

Another concern teachers have is that students with failing grades all three quarters can hustle and receive a passing grade in the few weeks before final marks are recorded. The system sanctions that kind of stampede because it doesn't want too many failing students. Bennett had noted that disturbing occurrence in her initial letters to me. "I think it says what the expectations are," she said.

That made me think of an e-mail I got from a sad dad whose daughter graduated with honors from a suburban high school but was blown out of her college dream because she couldn't compete with foreign students. They come to this country on fire with their ability to learn. As Vanja Selimbegovic, a Bosnian refugee in Beatrice McKindra's sophomore class, told me, school in the United States is far less demanding than her school in Bosnia. Here she was taking seven courses and had hardly any homework; in Bosnia she would have had 17 classes and would have been swamped with work. And so foreign students end up wrecking the grade curve and opportunities for many of our poorly prepared American kids.

This just goes to underscore what Stephanie G. Robinson and others have said: if communities want to raise student performance, critical thinking and analytical skills, they must support national standards in education beyond today's underfunded mandates and empty buzz phrases such as No Child Left Behind. Mandates in such initiatives, which focus on grading schools based on standardized test scores alone, add to the joke that politics makes of education. Such political hot air makes it impossible for America to keep up with the rocket-science pace of global competition because our schools end up graduating students with horse-and-buggy skills.

Company supervisors already contend with high school and college graduates who are ill-equipped for jobs. They have told me that, like the ninth-graders mentioned earlier, too many employees are putting up "Ricki Lake"- and "Jerry Springer"-type resistance when pushed to do good work. These media-inspired behaviors are now so pervasive that they have spilled over into all parts of society and are accepted, in some cases embraced, and too often highly valued.

Business people had also encountered young enemies of high academic standards when they had gone into schools to push students to reach for excellence now if they want good jobs in the future. Many said the verbal assaults they faced made them leery about ever returning to a classroom.

A similar "verbal assault" that Beatrice McKindra received from her students and that I wrote about in the column **"Employers will shun students who shunned writing lessons"** cited above prompted me to give the kids a reality check. I wrote that

> The rules of good English conflict with the way many of them have spoken all their lives. That's why no school district in the country should follow the Oakland, California, school board's lead in pandering to Black English, or Ebonics.
>
> Unlike French, Spanish, Latin or Japanese, Ebonics has no rules. I don't know of a teacher who would diagram sentences that read: "We still be doin' that," or, "They ain't nothin' t' me."
>
> How would Oakland teachers conjugate the verbs and make the lesson compelling to students who live in worlds of double negatives? One of the goals of education is to teach kids how to communicate so they'll be successful in life—not reinforce failure.
>
> Ebonics is one form of communication, but students

163

who use it at all times won't get far in our competitive global economy. I told McKindra's kids that their wise-cracking in class had become too much for me to stomach.

I told the students that jobs go to people who prove they'll best represent companies' interests. Regardless of the work, employees who fail on little things such as double negatives, misspellings or incorrect verb usages won't be trusted with important tasks.

They won't get promotions or raises. Eventually they'll get fired. They'll fall prey to the predators in the business world who'll also find profit in their academic deficiencies.

I told the students that McKindra was just trying to build them up now so they wouldn't fail in the future. If students learn the language of the business world, they'll be successful and get the respect they deserve.

They'll also get the things they'll need in life instead of being frustrated and manipulated by people who live to take advantage of folks of all colors who are lightly educated.

Parents, students, businesses, taxpayers, civic and faith leaders, and educators should expect only high standards in education; they shouldn't settle for less. None of us can afford to plunge to a deplorable level even though that apparently is where some people in America want us to go. We need to push the students to a higher level of performance, even when they balk. Because by resisting the higher standards, students are in effect defending their right to be ignorant.

Furthermore, low-performing students will ruin a school's reputation and trip all students if they try to rely on their alma mater's standing for college or jobs. A case in point lies across the state line in Missouri, where in 1999, the Kansas City School District lost its accreditation from the state board of education. That left the school district, its graduates, students preparing for college and city officials wringing their hands over what to do. (The district has since earned "provisional" accreditation.)

Students, therefore, need to devote their energy to striving for
excellence, supported by parents, teachers and the community.
Thank goodness some members of the community and most
teachers never give up trying to push students to achieve beyond
general low expectations. For example, some people who followed this series of columns called, wrote letters and sent e-mail
in hopes of enhancing the learning process. They sent me applications for workshops, seminars and scholars programs, which I
forwarded to educators and students at Washington High. The
applications came from professional groups and universities. One
was from Dr. Renate Mai-Dalton at The University of Kansas
Multicultural Business Scholars Program. She was among the
persons who promised Washington High School students Kresha
Crift and Eva Tilford early exposure to business careers and offered teachers greater access to multicultural education programs.
Such community involvement is encouraging and essential.

Dennis Bobbitt, whose 7:25 a.m. advanced placement American
government class I sat in during my "senior year" at Washington
High, showed me a teacher's dedication to high standards. I wrote
about it in a column headlined **"Pressure, heat routine during
class."**

Bobbitt knows the seniors have no time to chill or relax.
This school year is their gun lap.

They'll have to pour every ounce of their academic energy into their final year of high school and maintain that
scholastic momentum to enter the faster lanes of college
next fall. On Monday, just one week into the semester,
Bobbitt already had his 17 and 18 year olds taking an hour-
long pre-ACT college entrance English test.

"This is just to let you know how to get prepared and let
you know where you are," he said.

The 10-page, 75-question test was tough. The oppres-
sive heat in the classroom wilted Sarah Finney, who told
me afterward that she nearly fell asleep during the exam.

"This test is for your benefit," Bobbitt said. "It won't affect your grade in this classroom."

After students scored their papers, he advised those who answered half or fewer questions correctly to use his classroom computer to upgrade their English skills. Students should aim for high ACT scores. Each point is priceless in inching students toward admittance to better colleges and awards in scholarships, grants and loans.

Bobbitt had a student hold up a handout that he'd given earlier, showing how she had highlighted the most pertinent material. He wanted everyone to get into that text-marking habit.

He also advised students to bring a spiral notebook to class because he'll be reviewing their note-taking ability. It's to get them into good college-level study habits for the day when no one'll watch and no one'll care.

The students last week had turned in papers comparing the 1776 Declaration of Independence with the 1963 Martin Luther King Jr. "I Have a Dream" speech. Bobbitt read the best essays, telling how each enduring document still embodies great visions for a better America.

Students who hadn't turned in their papers were admonished. Others who editorialized were cautioned.

"Take yourselves out of the loop when you're writing," Bobbitt said. "Answer the questions that are posed to you. Your teachers are not looking for your personal opinions."

He told me he's expecting 90 percent of his students to take the advanced placement exam in May and receive college credit for the course. Positive peer pressure, Bobbitt said, will propel them to succeed in his class.

"I've got the best of what we have to offer at Washington High," Bobbitt said. "I want all these kids to be focused on excelling."

The dumbing down of our young people is an unacceptable trend that needs to be reversed. Merely requiring more frequent standardized testing isn't the answer; the entire system of schooling and the broader view of education and its importance for our nation's future need to be carefully examined. Only if we can promote critical and analytical thinking over multiple choice/multiple "guess" skills; create community opportunities for greater, more diverse intellectual stimulation of our young people; turn off or tune out the hype; and get parents, teachers, administrators and students actively involved in raising the bar, will we succeed in reaching genuinely higher standards and achievement — combating what West called the "anti-intellectual culture." Without consciously pursuing goals beyond higher test scores, our students will find it harder and harder to compete in a global setting.

Part IV
Chapter 7
Enriching Education

Teachers have to make learning more interactive, attention grabbing and richer. That includes bringing in outsiders, multicultural materials, multimedia methods and putting students in touch with every real world connection educators can find. Just lecturing and covering the material doesn't pass muster in getting today's children to learn.

"*I* can't compete with their jobs!"

With those words American government teacher Dennis Bobbitt expressed his concern about just one distraction in the torrent that teachers have to work against to get and keep children's attention in today's classrooms. Besides minimum wage work, which robs students of time for sleep, exercise, family activities, community service, church and homework, the negative influences that young people bring with them from outside the schools include staying up late to watch television and problems at home. Because of kids' late-night TV habits, they can't remain awake in class let alone focus on what's being taught. In addition, they can't help but carry into schools their families' financial troubles, abuse, neglect and divorce.

Then there are the distractions that have been pushed into the schools by corporations: the candy, cakes, soda pop, juice drinks and gum that are allowed in classrooms because junk food vending machines line the schools' hallways. And there are also those time-honored distractions that teachers have had to battle for centuries: talking in class, passing notes, daydreaming, and looking out the window into space or out the doorway into the hall.

Faced with these problems, teachers have had to become incredibly creative to get students to embrace the lessons of the day. They can no longer use exclusively what Paulo Freire calls "the 'banking' concept" of education (72). Freire defines this as "an act of depositing, in which the students are the depositories and the teacher is the depositor" (72). Often students will ignore teacher "depositors" because kids have become deadened to what educators have to say and how they present the material. So instead teachers rely on other ways of helping children *discover* what they need to know in order to advance successfully to the next grade. Educators should encourage their students to pursue what Freire refers to as a "restless, impatient, continuing, hopeful inquiry . . . in the world, with the world, and with each other" (72).

In order to do this, teachers tap into the many resources available to them. These include guest speakers, theater productions, field trips, videos, CD-ROMs, music, peer group activities and interactive classroom projects. Such a multimedia, multicultural approach shows students the intricate web whose strands connect the different subject areas. I saw many of these activities being used during my tenure at Washington High School and witnessed how they enriched everyone's understanding of the material being studied.

Students' "restless, impatient, continuing, hopeful inquiry" became crystal clear when Beatrice McKindra's class decided it wanted to investigate the Harlem Renaissance. I tried to capture their enthusiasm and their ensuing discoveries in a column headlined, **"Teens thrive on spirit of discovery."** They were engaged in a teens-teaching-teens project that

> yielded new excitement about learning with a multicultural flair. Famous author Langston Hughes provided the spark.
>
> The 15- and 16-year-old students got turned on by the power of his poetry and the works of other black authors.
>
> "They made sense," Neosha Collier said. "The last stories we read, they reminded me of my grandma—the way they were talking.
>
> The students wanted more.
>
> "They said, 'Couldn't we do something?'" McKindra said. "I said, why not research that time period?"

169

The 1920s era that produced an abundance of talented African Americans was the Harlem Renaissance. McKindra's kids eagerly researched the period at the library and worked in several teams to give reports on their discoveries to the class.

It was an example of how multicultural studies shouldn't be forced into black, Hispanic, Asian American and Native American month or week ghettos. The literature and accomplishments of America's diverse people inspire excitement among students year-round.

"To sum it all up, we have black history now and then we will have it again in February," Deavon McWashington said.

"I didn't know the Harlem Renaissance even existed," Cori Ishmael said. "Then we started researching it, and it was interesting."

The students found that the Harlem Renaissance was one of the most important periods in African-American history. It blossomed from slavery, the Civil War, Reconstruction, broken reparation promises of 40 acres and a mule, widespread oppression after World War I and the first great migration of black people from farms in the South.

Harlem became the mecca for many black people. It was where African-American stars blazed the brightest. The creativity among artists, inventors and black activists was inspiring.

The 1920s also was a major period of national prosperity. African Americans then, as now, benefited greatly from the country's long stretch of economic intoxication with wealth.

The research teams did class reports on education, politics, fashion, nightclubs and poetry. Courtney Bettis, William Hawkins, Kresha Crift and Jaison Jones focused on jazz, plays and literature. Their research included great artists such as Louis Armstrong, Paul Robeson and Langston

Hughes.

Cori, Megan Randle, Corey Brinton and Brandon Mitchell studied nightclubs, where many black artists proved themselves. The students found that racism also infected some nightspots, where black people could entertain whites but they couldn't enjoy the shows themselves. "It was just a different type of slavery," Megan said.

Neosha, Shemeka Jackson, Steve Brown, Amelia Steele and LeAnna Watson explored the era's flashy fashions.

"It made it more vivid," Neosha said. "It makes your imagination run wild."

But library research is only one way students can explore the many characteristics of a time period. In some of Scott Milkowart's American history classes, students were encouraged to get to know the history of the 1960s and '70s through the music that era produced. It became clear during class discussions that young people especially used music to express their opinions about the world of their experience. In a column headlined, **"Listening to history sing loudly,"** I showed how Milkowart used music to help his students grasp the era.

Toussaint Turner and Rodney Porter played air guitar and chair-danced with others in one of Scott Milkowart's American history classes.

Room 114 rocked to oldies playing on a boom box.

"You learn about the times from listening to the music," Milkowart said. "The musicians will tell you what's going on."

The rock 'n' roll teachers in Milkowart's three classes included Jefferson Airplane, Jimi Hendrix, Creedence Clearwater Revival, Edwin Starr, Buffalo Springfield, Martha Reeves and the Vandellas, the Mamas and the Papas, the Beach Boys, Sam Cooke, the Temptations and the Jackson 5.

171

Milkowart even offered a counter to the counterculture by playing Merle Haggard's "Okie from Muskogee." The tunes were part of the multimedia learning, which makes history come alive for kids today.

The students listened to the lyrics and talked about the messages in the music.

"Young people were doing things that were against the norms of society," Milkowart said of the Vietnam War protests, the civil rights activism and the women's movements of the '60s and '70s.

"They didn't want to fit into the establishment."

The rebellion grew from the '50s against the generations that had served in two World Wars and suffered through the Great Depression. "But young people wanted their voices to be heard, and I think that's true today," Milkowart said.

When asked about the themes in the artists' music, Rodney and Toussaint said they sang of peace, love, freedom, equality, protest, escape, drugs, sex, and the senselessness of violence and the Vietnam War.

"The sex and drugs are still in the music today, too," Toussaint said.

Milkowart told the class about Jimi Hendrix's prowess as a guitar player and then put "Hey Joe" on the boom box. Joseph Macklin wagged his head and played air guitar to the song.

Joseph explained afterward that Hendrix was singing about a man named Joe who shot his girlfriend and her lover and tried to flee. It underscored that domestic violence was a problem then just like today.

In a class on Friday, Stephen Branstetter brought in his tape so Milkowart could play Hendrix's "Star-Spangled Banner." Ronnie Gray also asked him to play "Voodoo Chile," which taught me something new.

Ronnie said that oldie opened TV wrestling matches. Students had heard the other counterculture tunes because the music protesting the establishment in their parents' day has been clipped to market products and add youth-appealing fury to movies, TV shows and even cartoons like "The Simpsons."

Dead rockers must be rolling over in their graves.

But Milkowart let me help frame the music with its real history. I photocopied pages of the '50s, '60s and '70s from my *World Almanac* and stapled them to *The New Rolling Stone Encyclopedia of Rock & Roll* biographies of artists the students studied. That way they could see the musicians were products of their time.

How many of today's young people, however, take "their time" for granted? How many are unaware of the lessons of the past that their day-to-day environment holds? How many know little or nothing about the richness of their community and its place in history? It is educators who are charged with helping them discover past/present connections.

In *A People's History of the United States*, Howard Zinn writes, "If history is to be creative, to anticipate a possible future without denying the past, it should, I believe, emphasize new possibilities by disclosing those hidden episodes of the past when, even if in brief flashes, people showed their ability to resist, to join together, occasionally to win" (11). One of those "episodes of the past" that can offer "new possibilities" but which has remained hidden from many students in the Kansas City area is the Underground Railroad. Across the Missouri River from Parkville, Mo., are the Quindaro Ruins in Kansas City, Kan., now one of the best-known and biggest sites on the Underground Railroad. Through a field trip to the site, which I wrote about in a column headlined, **"Hands-on history on a hike,"** Washington High students and I were invited to smell, touch, see and hear the lessons of the present and the past.

The mud of 19th-century freemen and runaways walked with me hours after my field trip with students at Washing-

173

ton High School.

Senior English teacher Dennis Lawrence had invited me by e-mail to join him and about 120 of his students doing research that would tax all five of their senses. "The community is our text, and each student will be working on research projects in the community, which will be posted on the Web site they will create," Lawrence wrote.

"There are no books they can consult for this," he said.

I answered his invitation and spent an hour with the teens in the ruins of Quindaro. The walk through the cemetery and old town were new experiences for me and students in the Class of 1999 at Washington High.

Lawrence said that for about seven years he had taken seniors to old Quindaro, the 1856 town where runaway slaves found freedom.

At the old cemetery, April Wilson, LeAnna Watson and others noted the headstone markings and made pencil etchings from them on their notebook paper. Lawrence then took us on a hike through the old town, where steamboats used to dock. Quindaro quickly grew to a freeport town of 608 persons. It had a four-story hotel, more than 100 business and residential buildings, and a daily newspaper.

"It's real interesting to learn something new about your heritage that you'd not known," Martin Bass said. "I think they need to make it into a national park."

Such proposals have been widely discussed locally and nationally.

We got high on the sights, smells, sounds, feel and taste of freedom and history in the area. Planes flew loudly overhead.

Train whistles sounded on the track by the Missouri River, and the traffic roar on nearby Interstate 635 cut the still air. The highway like many in urban areas divides the community, making it inaccessible and vulnerable.

174

Some students knew too well the blight, abuse and neglect of the modern ruins of the northeast community around Quindaro Boulevard in Kansas City, Kan. The old town by the river, however, was the history they'd never been told.

"To me, this is about going back in time, knowing who did what so we can have what we have today," Marcus Harris said.

"It's a way to find out about the place where you live," Eric Hernandez said.

The Quindaro Ruins have survived total abandonment, nearly 150 years of decay, flooding, lawsuits and failed efforts to bury it with a landfill.

"It's very exciting," Ebony Gipson said. "But they've destroyed so much, there's not a lot for us to learn."

Lawrence pointed to the remains of a stone structure with a tunnel in back. A creek gurgled nearby. With financing it could have been developed into a tourist magnet.

But it's as if the area is still paying for its abolitionist past. It made Jeanine Hegwood ask lingering questions: "How come nobody else taught us about this? Isn't this history important, too? What? Nobody cares about it?"

Lawrence's project succeeded in getting students to care about their community through their studies at Washington High School.

Lecturing—or "depositing"—alone cannot induce that kind of caring, which stimulates students to question, evaluate and learn about their world's past and present. Being able to experience first-hand, or visually and aurally revisit what others went through before them, and then think about and discuss the experience, allows students to shape, critically consider and reshape their own opinions. Such discovery generated lively and sometimes surprising discussions in the classroom.

On one such occasion, Scott Milkowart used the video "Rebel Without A Cause," starring James Dean and Natalie Wood, to give his American history students a taste of the '50s. In a column headlined, **"A real man can wear an apron,"** which I wrote about the students' reactions to the film, I noted that

their discussion got hung up on the male and female roles in the video.

The students split along gender lines. The trigger involved Dean's seeing his dad in an apron cleaning up a mess he'd made carrying food to Dean's mom.

"His dad was a wuss for taking his mom something to eat and cleaning up the floor," Ron Gray said.

"That's woman's work!" another male student shouted. "He's supposed to be the head of the family."

Kresha Crift, who liked the video because it wasn't "a 'Leave It to Beaver' thing," responded: "First of all, there is no such thing as a man's or a woman's job. A job is a job."

But Steve Brown retorted, "Who's going to wear an apron and walk around the house like a woman?"

Krista Cunningham shot back: "Maybe he's secure in who he is as a man. Nowadays, you see a lot more women working, and the man is sitting at home. If you drop something on the floor, you've got to pick it up."

But a male student said, "All I know is she had him whipped."

"He lost his manhood," Steve added.

Milkowart looked stunned. "I didn't know this video would evoke so many deep-seated insecurities," he said.

Scott Milkowart and other skilled teachers use television and computer technology as the Trojan Horse that fascinated kids embrace. All sorts of surprises in information, knowledge and wisdom tumble out of the devices that students readily take in. It lets teachers have a fighting chance at conquering ignorance.

Television today talks to students more than anyone in their lives. We cannot discount the effect that television news, for example, has on children's sense of the world. They follow TV news, and it affects them. Bringing current events into the classroom can show the concrete application of textbook theory. Because students know what is going on around them, linking their knowledge of today to what their books say breathes life into seemingly moribund material. A column captured that under the headline, **"Caught up in the flow of history."**

> The unavoidable happened this week in Dennis Bobbitt's class.

> Independent counsel Kenneth Starr on Wednesday shipped sealed boxes of evidence against President Bill Clinton to the House of Representatives. Starr reported what he called 11 possible grounds for impeachment in Clinton's attempts to cover up an affair with former White House intern Monica Lewinsky.

> Bobbitt brought up the topic Thursday in his American government class. His seniors pounced on it. The news ignited their enthusiasm and gave context to otherwise dry textbook lessons.

> The students constantly surprise me with their current-events awareness and with how today's media cynicism affects their views.

> "Bill Clinton broke my heart," Bobbitt said.

> The intense discussion that followed mirrored the prevailing public view of Clinton's affair with Lewinsky. Students didn't think his actions constituted an impeachable offense, and they said he shouldn't resign.

> As long as he gets his job done in the White House, who cares? Antonio Garcia asked.

"Everybody's got problems," Shanell Downs said. Clinton broke his marriage vows. That's between him, his wife, Hillary, and their daughter, Chelsea. "It's not supposed to be in public."

Devon Bell added: "We don't need to get into his personal life."

Clinton obviously "didn't go to 'player university,'" where he'd have learned "the down low" of undercover relationships, Andrea Smith said.

Nannette Young said the Clintons jet around in a world far above ours, where abuse of power can seem inevitable. Tears from little people like us are better shed on anything else.

Bobbitt steered the class into his lecture on Abraham Lincoln's view of government and power. Students took notes: "Power is the possession of control over others. Power once acquired must be defended if it is to be maintained."

We wrote down the classic forms of government, oligarchy, autocracy and democracy, and classic economies, capitalism, socialism and communism.

Then Bobbitt broke the class into groups for a government-building exercise. I sat with William Hawkins, Jordan Steinmetz, Antonio, Andrea and Shanell. We picked a representative democracy to rescue our shipwrecked society.

With all of its human failings, it seemed like the best hope for us—just as it is for America today.

Making connections by using different instruments—books, lectures, videos, computers, TV, music, and field trips, among others—to stimulate learning also has the added benefit of tapping into students' different learning styles. In a column headlined **"Nurturing a feeling for history"** (see Appendix), I wrote that

Scott Milkowart used the multimedia setup in his classroom to give his students a more accurate picture of the many colors in the mosaic that we call America. To start off, he had his students watch the video "Eyes on the Prize," which focused on the Civil Rights Movement. The video most certainly helped his visual and auditory learners grasp the importance of the marches, the brutality, and the moving speeches by the Rev. Martin Luther King, Jr., Malcolm X and President Lyndon B. Johnson. He then reinforced the video with the book, *Free at Last: A History of the Civil Rights Movement and Those Who Died in the Struggle*, and had the students work in groups on reports, thus stimulating visual learning in his students. His earlier use of music to bring home the messages of the '60s and '70s undoubtedly helped his auditory learners. And the field trip to the Quindaro Ruins that Dennis Lawrence organized (and which I wrote about in the column **"Hands-on history on a hike"** mentioned above) offered the kind of hands-on experience that kinesthetic learners thrive on. Covering the students' learning styles by using the many tools available in today's high-tech educational environment helps teachers grab and keep kids' attention.

In a column headlined **"Learning to confront prejudice,"** I wrote about the many-pronged approach that I had seen Alice Bennett use during a semester of learning about power and prejudice. The last step in the process after many others was the students' final exam:

> The test was on Elie Wiesel's book, *Night*, which detailed atrocities that Nazis inflicted on Jews in World War II. But the lessons began the month before at the Coterie Theatre in Kansas City, Mo., where I sat with Bennett's ninth-grade English classes to watch the play *Anne Frank and Me*.

> The drama about a '90s girl's trip back to Nazi Germany as a Jew was heart-rending. I also saw how many of the students were moved as they watched a video, "The Holocaust: Through Our Own Eyes," and listened Monday to a two-hour lecture from Holocaust survivor Sam Nussbaum, whom Bennett brought in from the Midwest Center for Holocaust Education in Overland Park, Kan.

179

He talked about the horrors that he had had to endure, the losses he had suffered in seeing many family members and friends never return and the guilt he sometimes feels for having survived. His plumbing skills saved him. Even the Nazis with all of their self-inflated projections of superiority needed plumbers to keep their water and drain pipes working. The students and I hung on every word Nussbaum shared with us.

Such multiple approaches to teaching were what got the students to realize and accept the importance of the Holocaust in world history and to never forget, which is an ongoing wish of the global tragedy's many aging survivors.

The lessons on power and prejudice also have been hands-on for this interactive generation. Bennett's room once smelled of marker fluid because students used felt-tip pens to write their definitions of prejudice and stereotypes on large sheets of paper.

"Stereotyping is labeling a person without knowing the person," Joseph Macklin and Bobby Ford wrote. Prejudice, Brandon Mitchell and Mike Kepler wrote, is hatred for things and people who are different.

On another day, Bennett pinned large stars on some students and told the others that the teens with stars were Jews that day. She rewarded students without stars with candy for "ratting" on the misbehavior of teens with stars just as Nazis used commodities to get Gentiles to turn against Jews.

The students sold each other out with wild excitement. "Just as with our candy, can you begin to imagine how important it is to turn a family in if you are hungry or cold?" Bennett said.

It had a sense of the same famous "brown eyes/blue eyes" experiment that then-schoolteacher Jane Elliott used with her third-grade class in 1968 in an Iowa public school to get her all-white students to understand what diversity is all about. Her experiment followed the death of the Rev. Martin Luther King, Jr. I have heard Elliott, now a diversity champion, repeat in lectures in Kansas City that getting the children or adults labeled as inferior to wear collars was a method used in Nazi Germany on Jewish people. She also pointed out how close this country is to enacting such a thing in this country with minorities.

In her class, Bennett gave stars to other teens a day later and had them stand on brown sheets of paper to represent the isolated ghetto life of Nazi-era Jews, which Wiesel described in *Night*. Jessica Brinza was among the students given a star.

Nichole Burke moved into her desk. "Boy, how quickly your friend took over your house," Bennett said illustrating how the book told of Jews losing their property when the Nazis herded them into ghettos.

Bennett then had the students move from the brown to black paper taped to the classroom floor. It marked the shift from ghettos to cattle cars, which took Jews to concentration camps where 6 million of them died.

Bennett told me later that she was amazed that the students with and without the stars fell in line so willingly. None with stars tried to escape from the ghettos, and none left the tight confines of the cattle cars. Bennett's teens joked about what they and their friends had to endure.

But it was clear that the humor was their way of lightening the burden of the heavy exercise. I learned a lot from the experiment, too.

It showed me how trusting people are and how quickly they can be herded into complying with changes that are detrimental to others. It was one of the last lessons I picked up in Bennett's classes before summer vacation set us all free.

I only hope that the students were moved as much as I was by the experience and that they will always act against prejudice and abuse of power as they advance in age, grade and life.

Nudging students toward a greater, more complete grasp of the mountains of information they need to navigate is the challenge that teachers today face. The tried and true method of yesteryear—"depositing" by lecturing—is no longer enough. Teachers are almost *required* to use a wide variety of modern, high-tech, multimedia and multicultural resources to capture students' interest, keep them engaged and help them learn effectively.

When I visit elementary, middle and high schools, I try to help students understand the value and outcome of their education by showing them what their many distractions are "costing" them and impressing on them the need to take advantage of what they are being offered. I take what the students know and value— money—and use it to illustrate the point. I pull a $50 bill from my wallet and put it on the floor in front of them. I tell them that teachers do the same thing every day, daring students to pick up the $50 bill. That financial capital represents the intellectual capital that teachers should daily drop in front of each student. But the best teachers don't give the full $50 to each student all at once. They may put down $25 some days, $30 other days, and when they bring in guests or use interactive materials, another $15 might be added. The students' interactions with the teacher, the guests, classmates or the other materials boost the total to $50.

To illustrate the capital that accrues, I then put another $50 bill on the floor for each school day, so that there is a total of $250 in $50 bills on the floor in front of the class, representing the intellectual capital investment that students should have received from teachers for the week. The young people are always astounded that I would so casually "play" with so much money. Then I get the students to do the math: multiplied for the month, it's $1,000; for the school year it's about $9,000, or the per pupil amount that many school districts spend to educate each child. That's $9,000 in daily intellectual capital allotments of $50 bills that each student should have picked up and banked so that progressing into the next grade is easier and academic success is more certain.

Like most investments, this one, too, is slow to build, but it ultimately generates gains. Payback comes with college entrance exams, which are supposed to measure how much in intellectual capital students have accumulated and whether interest in what they have banked has accrued. High scores generally indicate that students have picked up a lot of intellectual capital during their academic careers. Low scores may be an indication that they didn't pick up much and that long-term deficiencies in the intellectual capital exchange between the students and their teachers prevented that banking from occurring. Colleges look for students who have the high scores—those who have presumably banked a lot of intellectual capital—then provide scholarships, grants and loans to pay for those students to continue their education.

It's here that the intellectual capital yields financial returns. Those students will likely continue to pick up a lot of intellectual capital in college, which impresses prospective employers. The yield, then, is in intellectual capital becoming financial capital in high paying jobs because of the properties students will likely display. Conversely, students who didn't pick up all of the $50 in intellectual capital end up paying their way through college, if they go at all and if they finish with a degree. Many struggle in low-wage jobs as companies deem them to have little to offer in intellectual capital that can help generate new intellectual properties.

The sad part of this is that too few kids are let in on this secret. The $50-bill analogy helps make tangible in terms familiar to young people their ability to shape their futures. The money trick, which excites children and young adults, takes what they value as extreme media consumers exposed to tremendous amounts of commercialism and marketing and links it to what they need to know about the short- and long-term outcomes of getting the most out of education. In close cooperation with their teachers and through the many methods and resources those teachers are now providing them with, students can and should fully capitalize on the wealth of experience and information at their disposal.

The changes that teachers have had to make in education in order to make it richer for their students are far-reaching. Think back to the image presented in the introduction of education as a skyscraper and imagine the process as that of the aging skyscraper being retrofitted with new wiring for high-speed Internet connections, new plumbing for water-saving, automatic faucets and self-flushing urinals and toilets, and energy-efficient lighting devices. If it's done right, the additions are marvelous enhancements to the superstructure: the traditional topics of reading, writing, math, English, history, geography, science, foreign languages, and the many other subjects and traditions that make up the concrete foundation of education are strengthened and enriched. The innovations might seem strange at first, might tax teachers' creativity, flexibility and energy, but the ultimate returns—a more modern, well-equipped skyscraper peopled with engaged and eager students—are well worth the effort.

Part IV
Chapter 8
The Rewards

Teachers are not the enemy. They are some of the best advo-cates our children have, and they need our undying guidance and support. Anything less sets our children, our schools and our community up for failure.

PORTRAIT:
Ruby Jeffries and
Christine McLennan

Hugs are symbolic for teens

Every morning at 7:05, Ruby Jeffries and Christine McLennan open their window and students line up in the hall before classes start.

Jeffries, an English teacher, and McLennan, a speech and reading teacher, peddle school supplies and snacks. I pass their minibazaar on the way to Scott Milkowart's American history class.

McLennan is the sponsor of Teachers of Tomorrow; Jeffries oversees the Key Club.

"It's for the kids," Jeffries said of working in the window.

"We get a chance to meet all the kids here," McLennan said Wednesday. "You build sort of a relationship that is not threatening, and I think it works."

The $3,000 they annually raise helps offset national and state club dues and enables the groups to make community donations. They also recruit volunteers. McLennan tapped me last month to read my daughters' Dr. Seuss books to kids at Douglass Elementary School on Read Across America Day.

I've found in studying with the Class of 1999 that such unsung, special efforts by teachers live in the margins with the praise or constructive comments they write on students' papers. But these are the hallways that make our schools unique and our kids successful.

"We tend to interact with the kids so much," Jeffries said. "Somehow they can't find it anywhere else."

A.C. Nielsen found that young people spend only 38.5 minutes per week in meaningful conversations with parents. Another survey showed that 80 percent of kids find it difficult or awkward to talk with parents about serious issues.

"It's just a time in society when you have to be so much more," Jeffries said of teaching. "You have to be their friend. You have to be their parent."

The thanks in these hallways of education happen in spontaneous hugs and heartfelt handshakes from students. "It's gratifying," Jeffries said.

I saw that in 1995, when Alice Bennett first invited me to study with the Class of 1999. The teens embraced her. The next year some hugged Beatrice McKindra, who let me study with the sophomores in her English class.

I've seen students shake Milkowart's hand. As a coach he often subs as a father figure.

I've shaken the young men's hands all three years I've been at the school. This year both the male and female students have surprised me with hugs.

Hugs are typical, Assistant Principal Mary Viveros said.

"It happens to me a lot," Viveros said. "I think when you're little, you're a little more huggable.

"It's tricky the other way, although there are times when you want to reach out and give teenagers a hug."

In the language of hugs, being cool and being tough evaporate. The students simply want to convey respect, thanks, kindness and closure, Bennett said.

"It's, 'I'm OK, you're OK,'" Bennett said. "It's, 'I'm no longer angry with you as the teacher. Please don't be angry with me as the student, and we survived the year.'"

"When they hug me, I hug them back."

Some of the most rambunctious students from all grades surprise Bennett with hugs. "I had one of the boys come up to me last week and put his arms around me and say, 'You can be my other mom,'" she said.

"I said, 'Kenneth, does this mean I have to feed you? Does this mean I have to do your laundry?'"

We both laughed about that in her classroom, which I revisited at Washington High School.

❖ ❖ ❖ ❖ ❖ ❖ ❖ ❖

*T*he Washington High School project yielded several lessons. One was I will never advocate eliminating the three-month vacation that teachers have. Those men and women who stand before our children five days a week, nine months a year need that time off to recover. I suppose teaching is like playing a professional sport. One has to psyche oneself up for the season and then for each brutal day of "the game." The three-month off-season is needed to rest, psychologically heal, and then get geared up for the next "season." Going back to school takes a lot of mental preparation.

I have been moved by the amount of extras teachers have brought into their classrooms. But teaching has never been and should not be a solitary experience. It's more of a facilitation in which teachers, students and other adults form a triangle of success for our children. I have been compelled time and again to take that message to adults outside of schools. Our children and teachers need other adults' time and commitment. We must, by our increased involvement in our schools, raise the achievement expectations that we have for our kids and our educators.

Someone told me once that we only have one set of children. We aren't keeping a better set at home waiting for better times. Therefore, we have to do all that we can for all of our kids now because they won't get a second chance at a good education. But unless parents do something about the problems of education, unless they support teachers, ask for homework and then work with kids as if they were homeschooling them; unless more people take an active interest in our children's schooling now and at all grade levels; and unless professionals share their expertise with and stimulate the interests of the students, our kids will continue to fail. And all of the material things that we as parents have wanted for our kids will be for naught. Our kids have got to be prepared each day of life to stand on their own two feet so they will be successful and productive as adults. But for that to happen we've got to step up and get involved more. It's the only way to end the war that's killing education for our children and threatening the betterment of our community.

I would like to see every community group get more involved in every school across America. For example, I would like businesses to sponsor annual potluck dinners at the schools to celebrate the education that those schools provide and to honor the teachers and students. It has to happen for the kids to see that education is vitally important to all of us.

But as Harvard Public Policy Professor Robert D. Putnam writes in his book, *Bowling Alone: The Collapse and Revival of American Community*, the opposite seems to be taking place. Putnam notes the decline in PTA membership. It has fallen from a high of 12.1 million members in 1961-62 to only 5.9 million members now. To quote Putnam, "one need not romanticize PTA meetings of the 1950s to recognize that many Americans nowadays are less involved with their kids' education" (57). Unfortunately, when parents and other adults are not more involved in the schools, it is not only the schools that suffer but the entire community as well.

To restore a sense of community, which is sorely needed, Putnam demonstrates the importance of social capital. By his definition, social capital is that sense of community and that sense of caring and trust that grows from people getting together to talk and share stories about their lives and their ideas (299). The alternative— isolation—isn't pretty. Teachers see it every day, and Putnam writes about that, too. Students who live in high-risk areas feel less connected to their communities, and their parents are less likely to trust anyone or to reach out for help. It's in that isolation that children suffer, educators are traumatized and gangs form to fill the social network void. Putnam writes: "Social capital matters for children's successful development in life. We can draw the same conclusion about the link between social capital and school performance. The quality of American education has been of growing concern in recent decades; in fact, many knowledgeable observers believe that public schooling has reached a crisis" (299).

Putnam finds that states such as North Dakota, Minnesota, Iowa and Nebraska with high social capital tend to have children who do better in school regardless of their family's income. States such as Missouri, Texas, Florida and Illinois with moderate levels of social capital have students who struggle to achieve, while low social capital states such as Mississippi and Louisiana have kids who barely have a future at all (297-99). Putnam adds that "the beneficial effects of social capital persist even after accounting for a host of other factors that might affect state educational success— racial composition, affluence, economic inequity, adult educational levels, poverty rates, educational spending, teachers' salaries, class size, family structure and religious affiliation, as well as the size of the private school sector (which might 'cream' better students from public schools)" (299-300).

One of the benefits that I didn't foresee in my involvement at Washington High School was that it helped to boost the sense of caring, the social capital among students, teachers and people in the community. There was a gap that my involvement unintentionally filled, and that should be filled by neighborhood organizations, churches and businesses. The schools should be centerpieces of our communities, and people should be drawn to them. That craving for the community to embrace the schools came out in a column headlined, **"Celebrate to avoid disaster."**

Air Force Sgt. John Jacobs looked around the cafeteria at Washington High School.

People were seated at every table. Good food prepared by his co-workers on the faculty made the evening scrumptious. Turnout, said Jacobs, who teaches ROTC at Washington High, was better than expected at the First Annual Parent Hospitality Night last month, where chili was on the menu.

I saw him again Thursday night in the school cafeteria. The lunchroom was packed with more than 700 people at the Second Annual Washington High School Air Force Junior ROTC Awards Banquet and Ceremony. Turnout at the ROTC awards dinner this year was twice as large as in 1998.

It was wonderful to see so many family members, friends, educators and military personnel attend the positive event.

It offered hope for a nation suffering despair over the massacre at Columbine High School in Colorado. Two students last week killed 12 classmates, a teacher and themselves. They wounded many others.

Last week was better here. After the ROTC dinner, we moved to the gym. Students dressed in ROTC uniforms stood at attention along the hallway. In the gym the audience sat in the bleachers as students in blue uniforms did precision drill team marching. Video and still cameras captured it. The place also thundered with applause as the students received awards.

Witnessing such events and the pride on so many faces has been a fabulous part of following the Class of 1999 at Washington High School.

Last month's chili supper was a new outreach. Students, educators and family members embraced it, making the school a centerpiece of the community. "We need more events like this," Jacobs said at that dinner.

I saw Dennis Bobbitt at the chili supper and at Thursday's ROTC banquet. I'm studying with seniors in his American government class now.

Scott Milkowart was at the chili supper. He let me study with the juniors in his American history class a year ago.

I sat with Beatrice McKindra at the chili supper. She let me into her sophomore English class in 1996-97.

Alice Bennett was the first to invite me to sit in her freshman English classes in 1995. She got me seats with the other teachers. She didn't make the chili supper. Bennett had undergone surgery, but she's OK now.

We often forget that teachers are people, too, with their own families and personal dramas. But I've also learned from attending all three dinners that educators, parents and students cook really well.

Sarah Finney, in her ROTC uniform, helped serve drinks to people. Her mom, Susan Findley, and grand-mother, Dorothy Findley, cheered for her at the ROTC awards ceremony. They also savored the evening with her at the chili supper.

Nannette Young, operations group commander of the school ROTC unit, brought her parents, James and Chris-tine Young, and other family members to the ROTC event. They were so proud of Nannette, whose leadership earned unprecedented honors for her and the school.

I was happy for all of the ROTC seniors and let Sarah, Nannette, Jerry Cheray Whitlock, Sarah Cole, Jessica Brinza and Nichole Burke know it.

Jacobs is right. More events like these need to take place to reconnect Washington High School with the community and the community with Washington High School.

Every school should have such celebrations. It's better than waiting for a new disaster to erupt and then wonder-ing why.

ROTC's involvement in the schools is important. But it must be balanced by other groups and individuals having a greater pres-ence in schools, in assisting educators and in directing the lives of young people. Caring adults in the community act as mentors. Their careers become real world examples of the jobs young peo-ple might seek. Adults' civic involvement also instructs young people on what they, too, must do. But the No Child Left Behind law muddles things. The law that President George W. Bush backed gives military recruiters greater access to young people, establishing a huge institutional imbalance. In effect, it chases away other adults from being more involved in our schools. When this happens, the schools lose, the students lose, educators lose and the community loses. These are new losses in the war to educate our children. It then becomes just one of many failed wars, such as the war against crime, the war on drugs, the war against pov-erty, the war against terrorism. We can't afford the losses, especially in educating our children.

The law went into effect in 2002, requiring public and private high school administrators to let military recruiters onto campuses that receive money under the Elementary and Secondary Education Act. Only private schools with religious objections to military service are exempt. Schools that refuse admittance to military recruiters could lose federal financing. That is not an attractive option for any school district in these tough economic times of program cuts, large class sizes and teacher shortages.

A joint letter from Defense Secretary Donald Rumsfeld and Education Secretary Rod Paige told schools to "work closely with military recruiters" (Hutcheson). The law requires that schools turn over the names, addresses and telephone numbers of juniors as well as graduating seniors. The only way for kids to avoid getting the recruitment sales pitch is if parents tell school administrators not to surrender students' personal information to military officials.

And military recruiters are taking full advantage of their special privileges: they're hanging out at high schools. But I'd rather see college recruiters discussing career options with students, enticing them to sign up for universities. I'd also prefer to see banks, credit unions and people with scholarship and grant applications milling about school lobbies providing young people with the financing they need to get to college and graduate with good jobs. If those adults were as aggressive as the military recruiters, our kids would have a more peaceful and productive future. Our country would, too.[*]

Students need to see and hear as many differing viewpoints as possible so that they can grow into informed and thinking adults. There are many types of careers that young people can pursue. Their exposure to the possibilities should never be overwhelmingly lopsided, favoring one small but powerful sector of society.

---

[*] The full text of the column headlined, "Pushy recruiters descend on high schools," that contains this and more information is in the Appendix.

In the same way, because we live in a multicultural society, we must make sure our students are exposed to the richness if its diverse cultures and ideas.

To that end, having a culturally, civically and commercially mixed population of adults in the schools is desirable and even necessary. But to hold kids' interest, schools also have to incorporate a more multicultural curriculum so that it appeals to all students. The kids need to see successful people who look like them in their textbooks, their lessons and their classrooms. They need a diverse group of role models exposing them to the challenges and triumphs of as many ethnic groups as possible. A column in the Washington High series headlined, **"The old challenge is with us still: Triumph over mediocrity"** brought that out.

Alice Bennett let me share some of my favorite poems and passages with her students.

It seemed appropriate to put Shakespeare on hold for some literary gems of African-American authors in honor of Black History Month.

Sharing black literature opened my eyes to a universe of new things. First I got to see what it was like to present the same material four different times before bells in the hallway emptied the room.

I lived Bennett's daily challenge of trying to find fresh ways to present ages-old material. But I also had to pitch it so that the diverse classes could see themselves and modern-day America in the rich black literature.

My goal—like Bennett's daily charge—was to infect the students with my germs of excitement about the school, the classwork and them. I saw that teachers get their thrills in seeing young faces light up with a new enthusiasm for learning and in students like Deaudrey MacDonald, 15, staying after class to say thanks.

In the 8:30 a.m. class, I had Monai Myers, 15, read Langston Hughes' "Mother to Son" aloud. The dialect threw her and made it difficult for her to read, but she managed to get the meaning across to her classmates:

Well, son, I'll tell you:
Life for me ain't been no crystal stair.
It's had tacks in it,
And splinters,
And boards torn up,
And places with no carpet on the floor --
Bare.
But all the time
I'se been a-climbin' on,
And reachin' landin's.
And turnin' corners,
And sometimes goin' in the dark
Where there ain't been no light.
So, boy, don't you turn back.
Don't you set down on the steps
'Cause you finds it's kinder hard.
Don't you fall now --
For I'se still goin', honey,
I'se still climbin',
And life for me ain't been no crystal stair.

I asked Joseph Macklin, 15, what it meant. "Life is going to be hard," he said. "But don't just give up."

Marcus Harris, 15, added, "It's about growing up and making something out of yourself."

Timisha Tolefree, 14, said she could see herself in the poem, but also could see her parents, who want her to grow up strong, smart and beautiful. "It really told you a lot," she said.

I also showed the different classes a passage from Bebe Moore Campbell's book *Brothers and Sisters*. In Bennett's 9:20 a.m. class I had Megan Randle, 15, read it aloud.

A white bank employee, Mallory, was perplexed by Esther, a black co-worker. *Every once in a while, she had the inkling that Esther's seeming commitment to the bank wasn't anchored in dedication or even ambition; she was driven by darker forces, which Mallory couldn't fathom.*

I asked the students what they thought those "darker forces" were. Adrian Hutson, 15, pegged them as the drive within Esther to be better.

I expanded that, telling the kids that "black" or "dark" normally have negative meanings, but not in this case. To me those "darker forces" spoke of black ancestors, black heritage, and one enslaved or oppressed generation pushing the next to achieve beyond what it was able to accomplish.

Retired Gen. Colin Powell put it this way in a speech to the National Association of Black Journalists in 1989: Unprecedented advances of African-Americans were only possible because each new generation had been pushed and stood on the strong, black shoulders of giants.

It's a classic American tale of people achieving despite the odds and setting records that they then push other generations to surpass.

Bennett passed me a note that touched my heart: "Thank you for the lesson today—and for the grace under which it was administered. I hope I can take that back to my family and students."

Because of what I learned that day, I should have thanked her.

But students' work doesn't end with the final bell for classes; therefore, involvement can and must also take place outside of school. Partnering with an adult on her or his job for even a few hours can be an invaluable experience for kids as well as for their "partner." And this is another way to get involved, perhaps for those who are reticent to go into the schools. In my case, for instance, students sometimes call to ask whether they can shadow me for a day as part of a class assignment. It happens to newspaper people and, as a community service, many of us often comply. Such a request during my time at Washington High School enabled me to give my "job shadows" what they needed and gain from their observations. Community service that benefits education is never a chore—just a bonus for everyone involved because of the many learning experiences that such extra efforts yield. The following Washington High column, **"Teenagers get a lesson in learning as partners in education,"** is a great example.

Katie Galvin and Brie Cable shared their impressions with me about Alice Bennett's classes.

The 16-year-old juniors from O'Hara High School in Kansas City, Mo., and I participated in the South Kansas City Chamber of Commerce's Partners in Education program. I had been involved in the partnership for years as an editor at *The Kansas City Star*. Some of the earlier students who had shadowed me had gone on to my alma mater, the University of Missouri-Columbia School of Journalism, graduated and gotten jobs in the news industry. On this morning, Galvin and Cable joined me on one of my weekly visits to Bennett's freshman English classes. Washington High School was about 40 miles away on the other side of town for them and me, too.

Galvin and Cable want to be journalists, so I gave them pens and notebooks from *The Kansas City Star* and asked for their observations as older teenagers about Bennett's classes.

Bennett's students were writing in journals in a lesson designed to help them steer their lives in a positive direction. Galvin liked that. So did Cable. "Everyone should be thinking about what they want from life, not only focusing on the day to day," Cable noted.

Students had to write essays on places they'd like to visit, sports they'd like to star in, what they want to be famous for, where they'd like to live, what they'd do with $1 million and changes they'd make if they were the U.S. president. Bennett also told the students she wanted them to come up with motivational thoughts to share with the class.

"I firmly believe that if you pollute your own space with violence on TV and in music, if you pollute it with hatred, if you pollute it with negative thoughts, that's what you become," Bennett said. "If you take your space and fill it

197

with positive thoughts and love, then that's what you become."

One inspirational thought cruised across the classroom
computer screen: "A candle loses no light when lighting
another." On one board "Put Downs" was in a circle with a
line drawn through it.

Cable and Galvin gave those things high marks. "I
thought the teacher was neat," Cable said.

"I liked all the inspirational things she had around the
room," Galvin said.

Cable also called the computer "a luxury that we don't
experience at a little Catholic school like O'Hara."

Cable and Galvin noted the relaxed classroom atmosphere, where students chewed gum, ate candy, studied or
moved around.

Galvin also was intrigued by the matching composition
notebooks, which she said "shows some type of uniformity
and discipline for the class."

She and Cable noted the unique self-expression in Bennett's students' clothes, compared with uniforms at their
school. They also noticed that the students worked well together, compared with the cliques and separateness of
many teens at their school.

They liked the racial diversity at Washington High
School, which existed without tension. "People get along
better at Washington," Cable said. They showed respect
for the teacher and for one another.

The girls were impressed that the freshmen were reading *Lord of the Flies*, which Galvin and Cable said they
didn't study until their sophomore year in honors English.
But they were disturbed by the misspellings, grammatical
errors and low grades on tests, which Bennett shared with
me.

Students in private school take education more seriously, Cable and Galvin said. They frowned on a girl writing her name with her boyfriend's on her hand. They thought that was immature.

Galvin, who lives in the more racially and ethnically diverse Northeast Kansas City, Mo., also thought Bennett's students were a lot like teens where she lives, compared with those at her more homogeneous south Kansas City school.

In the suburbs, students focus on what to do during the weekends. In the city, they're more watchful of things in their environment, and they're more worried about their safety, Galvin said.

After class I took the girls to *The Kansas City Star* for a tour and then to the Partnership lunch. It was a full day, and they gave me new information to digest about Bennett's classes.

Katie Galvin and Brie Cable saw what other teens' school day experiences were like while observing and learning from their exposure to my everyday work. Likewise, many students at Washington High School often surprised me by stripping away my veneer of "invisibility." Their questions about my work caused me to exit my observer status. I always greeted such unexpected attention openly. Such encounters were different and even fun as expressed in the column **"The bonds are growing all the time."**

Sometimes Beatrice McKindra's kids study me at Washington High School.

During a rare lull in McKindra's sophomore English class, Brandon Mitchell sat at a student desk near me to discuss his observations. He had started watching me in 1995-96 when he was a freshman in Alice Bennett's English class.

I went to McKindra's room in 1996-97. Brandon wanted to know how I got enough material for columns when McKindra didn't move students into a circle for group discussions as Bennett did.

199

I praised him for being so observant. But I said that, just like the students, I had to adapt to Bennett's and McKindra's different teaching styles.

Being an old beat reporter helped. Those skills enabled me to cover politics, the police, the courts and government.

For the last two years, they've helped me show what takes place in the education of our kids. Washington High School just happens to be the setting.

I told Brandon that what I couldn't get in class, I picked up by calling students at home, staying after school and doing extra work.

Another example of the kids outing me was in a column headlined, **"A shared experience in education"**:

Jeanine Hegwood stayed after class to satisfy her curiosity.

"I've been wondering what you've been writing in that notebook," said Jeanine, one of Beatrice McKindra's first-hour sophomore English students. Jeanine smiled, not knowing whether she was asking me to divulge too much. I had learned that Jeanine was skilled at stealthily watching and then unexpectedly confronting and unnerving people with the toughest questions. It was a trick good reporters used. I did it when I was pressing sources for information, and I'd been the editor of some of the best reporters in that game.

I smiled, too, because I knew I couldn't brush Jeanine off.

Assassinating a student's curiosity would be a crime like killing a mockingbird. Jeanine and her classmates knew that from studying Harper Lee's classic novel, *To Kill a Mockingbird.*

The book also caused them to have greater expectations

of adults. That's a good thing that they've learned in school.

It's also why I didn't mind reviewing what I had jotted down with Jeanine. Wanting to know is the first step in learning.

Through these and many other encounters I had, I inevitably discovered that none of the students I got to know at Washington High School was slow or incapable of learning. As we became better acquainted, the students enthusiastically shared their many activities and achievements with me. I showed this in the continuation of the column I cited above, **"The bonds are growing all the time."**

Brandon Mitchell and I started communicating this year via e-mail about his interest in computers, his friends and his love for music. His was the first of hundreds of e-mail messages that I have collected and continue to receive from students in the Class of 1999 at Washington High School.

Brandon started playing alto sax in fifth grade and has since learned other instruments. He was in a small band class last school year and in marching band this year.

"Playing at all the football and basketball games is a blast," Brandon wrote. "Next year I am going to be in jazz band, a new experience."

I found Jeanine Hegwood, Sarah Finney and Devon Bell performing in the band when I went to see Joseph Macklin and Steve Brown play on the Washington High basketball team. I didn't know that LaToya Watson was a cheerleader until then.

The girls in McKindra's class wanted me to know that they play basketball, too. MyKie DeGraftenreed, who sometimes wears her ROTC uniform, is a point guard for the girls' team.

Keasha Cannon pointed to her team picture on a poster

taped to McKindra's classroom door when I asked her earlier this school year how she injured her knee. She wore a leg brace after she suffered an injury playing basketball.

Alicia Johnson, Vanja Selimbegovic and Kresha Crift stay energized, striving for straight A's. I've seen school pride in April Wilson, Krista Cunningham and Eric Hernandez, who've shown me their new Class of '99 school rings.

Christopher Thoele showed me his Quill and Scroll pin, which he earned as sports editor for *The Washingtonian*, the school newspaper. Corey Brinton, Michelle Hyde and Sarah Finney brought in their swim team pictures for me to see.

William Hawkins told me he plays on the tennis team. Tiauda M. Taylor runs track. Aaron Halloway plays football, and so does Terry Wheat.

I got to know Terry last year along with Marcus Harris, who stops me in the halls so we can talk about his progress as a wrestler. I also ran into Marcus at Welborn Elementary School. He wore a Washington "Peer Leader" T-shirt, and little kids looked up to him at a career day.

Marcus and his classmates don't get graded on the extras that fill their lives. But those things add to their education and bond them to the school, community and each other.

My repeated presence in and outside the classrooms allowed me as an adult to see what teens are capable of and to throw out some of my own stereotypes and misimpressions. The richness of my own involvement will never fade in my memory. But I sometimes felt that even the time I invested and the things I did were not quite enough. I brought that out in the other column mentioned above, **"A shared experience in education."**

I stared out the classroom windows while McKindra's kids quietly concentrated on their final exams. Spring flowers had bloomed in what was once fall's brown playing fields.

McKindra's kids were maturing, too. Someone had written "JUNIORS!" on the chalkboard. Friday was their last day as sophomores. They'll return in the fall as upperclassmen.

I've been with the students up to seven times a month this school year, and on each occasion I've wished I had more time and things to give to McKindra and her kids. I couldn't give them money or logo-laden material things.

Ethics policies at *The Kansas City Star* prohibit me from crossing those lines. But what I tried to give the maturing students were things that would inspire them, enhance their well-being, boost their curiosity, accelerate their desire to be lifelong learners and let them know that adults really do care.

Bennett and McKindra in the last two years have enabled me to sit in student desks to learn from them and their pupils. Like the teachers, I've found that I'm hopelessly hooked on the narcotic called education.

McKindra let me join class discussions to connect literature the students studied with current events. She also let me divide the class one day in February so the students could compete in a Black History Month knowledge game that I bought just for them. That was fun.

Some people who've followed this two-year, intermittent series of columns on those enriching experiences have called, written letters and sent e-mail in hopes of enhancing the learning process. They've sent me applications for workshops, seminars and scholars programs, which I forwarded to educators and students at Washington High.

The applications came from professional groups and universities. They promised students early exposure to journalism and business careers and offered teachers greater access to multicultural education programs.

Kresha Crift told me this week that she'd been accepted into one of the college prep programs. It felt great to help

connect her with an opportunity that she might not have
otherwise had.

The students and teachers have been kind enough to
share their microcosmic worlds of adolescence, high
school and education with me. Going over notes and opening new doors to future learning have been my gifts to
them.

The rewards I reaped from getting involved in the everyday
school life at Washington High School have been many and invaluable, as I've tried to show above. But my involvement also
reminded my friend, SuEllen Fried, founder of the Stop Violence
Coalition, of another benefit which is called the Hawthorne Effect.
Researchers stumbled onto it by experimenting with lighting in a
manufacturing plant. They noted that when they increased the
wattage of light bulbs, worker productivity went up. They kept
increasing the lighting, and productivity kept rising compared with
other areas where the output remained constant. Then one wise
scientist decided that they should lower the wattage of the lighting
to see what might happen. They did, but worker productivity still
went up. They realized that lighting had nothing to do with increase in the workers' output. It was the fact that the workers
were being observed and measured. The researchers' expectations
were high, and the workers simply strived to meet those unbeliev-
able expectations. This goes back to what I mentioned at the beginning of this book: when students and teachers are observed, all
tend to rise to a higher level of performance *because of the outsider in the classroom.*

Another argument for taking an active interest in our students
and our schools is that there are definite downsides to *not* being
involved in schools, *not* paying close attention to young people.
Through not knowing what the students are really like, many people draw erroneous and damaging conclusions. I found, for example, that despite their brilliance and their successes, students from
urban schools still get slammed against the jagged rock walls of
prejudice and stereotypes constructed and diligently maintained in
our mostly segregated metropolitan community. As a black columnist who grew up in inner city St. Louis, I've long known this

to be an all-too-American tradition. It hurt me and my peers, but it seemed even more appalling to watch this bigotry get set up to limit the growth of innocent young people who only see the world through the lens of unbridled potential and supersized idealism. I couldn't allow the horrible ignorance among others to go unaddressed. To do so would give it sanction to continue. Here is where community service for education and adult involvement in schools can forge badly needed change to tear down the longstanding walls blocking students' climb to success. That comes out in the column, **"Geographic prejudice hurts dreams."**

Corey Brinton's eyes beamed with excitement when she shared her news with me.

Before Scott Milkowart's American history class had started, Corey told me she'd been picked for a full-ride scholarship to study at Kansas City Kansas Community College.

Dale Shetler, director of choir and orchestra activities at the college, confirmed it. "We call them music department performance grants," he said.

Corey is a junior. She sings with the Washington Song-Cats and was thrilled that music had punched her ticket to college so early. "I was really happy, and I was proud," said Corey, 17, who plans to be a teacher or foreign language interpreter.

"She's quite an awesome child," said Julie Brinton, Corey's mother.

Kansas City Kansas Community College is about a mile from Washington High School. I've learned that it's where many of the teenagers plan to begin college.

Ronnie L. Gray, 16, said he'll follow in his older brother's footsteps to the community college. Ronnie wants to major in business in his plan to open a record company.

"College is the way to go," Ronnie said. "It's not enough for you to have a high school education anymore."

Kansas City Kansas Community College offers Washington High students a passport to dreams through good instruction at a great location.

But others don't have that vision. They see the college, Kansas City, Kan., and its residents as ugly stereotypes. That surfaced in a column Shawn Hutchinson, a student at Johnson County Community College in Overland Park, Kan., wrote as sports editor of his school's newspaper, *The Campus Ledger*.

Hutchinson put the prejudices on paper that too many people outside Wyandotte County harbor. He wrote that he went to Kansas City Kansas Community College to watch basketball games.

His make-believe script went downhill from there, describing the campus and Kansas City, Kan., as being filled with guns, violence, drugs and crime. He made the students seem like hoodlums living the thug life.

I've visited the Kansas City, Kan., and Johnson County campuses and have found both to be equally good and students committed to furthering their education. The difference is Johnson County Community College is in one of the nation's wealthiest areas, and Kansas City Kansas Community College is in one of this area's poorest.

What Hutchinson wrote feeds the Heartland's address-based class system with one upper-income community looking down on the good people in another.

Hutchinson last week apologized in his column for his "derogatory" remarks. Johnson County Community College President Charles Carlsen apologized to Kansas City Kansas Community College President Thomas Burke and Carol Marinovich, mayor of the Unified Government of Kansas City, Kan., and Wyandotte County.

But I worry about the students at Kansas City Kansas Community College and Washington High School. Who will apologize to them?

And when will the damaging acid rain that the students feel because of where they live stop so they can achieve their dreams of becoming productive citizens?

Another clear downside to not getting involved is that kids are left to their own devices as adults in effect surrender them to the media babysitter. The violence they pick up there in language, gunplay and car crashes socializes too many of them into believing that such things happen and are acceptable and—in some cases— worthy of praise in our community. Without adults offering counterbalancing voices of reason, the one-upmanship of media violence will reign unchecked as the way things should be. Two columns in the Washington High School project served to connect the dots telling why adult involvement in all schools is critically important. They were **"Radio show was eerily prescient"** and **"Let's block the rush to violence."**

Not enough people listened. On her KKFI-FM talk show Tuesday, Barbara Crist and I talked about the destructive mix of the media, youths, hate and violence. What freaked me out later was that the community radio program was broadcast about two hours before the shooting and bombing started at Columbine High School in Littleton, Colo.

That day and well into the night, I watched TV commentators on 24-hour news networks repeatedly ask how the tragedy could have happened.

It was executed by Eric Harris and Dylan Klebold on what would have been Adolf Hitler's 110th birthday. They had rooted their plan in the Nazi's brand of hate and slaughtered 12 of their classmates, a teacher and themselves; many others were injured.

Harris and Klebold wore swastikas and used computers to dig deeper into destructive subjects. Crist and I warned of a continuing emergence of such bloody massacres, planned by neglected youths who had access to guns and money and were overexposed to hatred and violence in the media.

207

I told Crist I'd heard Jane Elliott, a diversity guru, give her formula for raising racist, sexist, homophobic, violent and elitist children: Parents should put them in front of TVs. The sweet, vile lessons will ooze from the tube.

It's also self-perpetuating. The media feed children hatred and violence. Then the media benefit when the children later do hateful and violent things.

I gave a speech on that in May 1996 at the Learning Exchange. That was long before a 16-year-old boy on Oct. 1, 1997, horrified the nation, killing his mother and shooting nine students, two fatally, in Pearl, Miss.

Since then, we've logged seven national incidents of children killing classmates and an epidemic of youths taking guns, bombs and violence into schools. Educators at the Learning Exchange wanted to know about my first year at Washington High School in Kansas City, Kan.

I told them about that and more. Teens are still as they've been throughout time.

They're discovering themselves, rebelling against older people and learning. They still talk about the opposite sex, who's dating whom, teachers, parents, transportation hangups, sports, weekend activities, college, money and jobs.

What's different is that more media are chasing them now, grabbing their hands and leading many down dead-end roads of bad choices. At the same time, the young people have been abandoned by adults, churches and neighbors. Parents and all adults should be filling children's lives, listening, responding without belittling comments, asking and answering questions.

Instead, too many parents park their kids in front of TVs, computers and video games and overindulge them with things, when adult attention and time are the things that children truly need. We've put our children at risk by letting the media take over and talk the loudest in many of our homes.

The media voices socialize our children with a language

of meanness and violence. It bleeds into children's behavior.

Then people like Harris and Klebold act out what they've learned and become national media stars.

The problem can be arrested, I said three years ago at the Learning Exchange and this week on KKFI. People should frequently declare "media-free days" instead of just National TV-Turnoff Week. Then they could enjoy the rich company and conversations that real people have to offer.

Given sufficient and effective adult guidance and care kids can be sensitized to the negative media messages and can overcome them. This became clear during thoughtful class discussions students had with their teacher Dennis Bobbitt and which I highlighted in the column, **"Let's block the rush to violence."**

President Clinton on Monday met with the nation's top educators, entertainment executives, religious leaders and gun industry officials for a youth violence summit at the White House.

But the lofty talks prompted by the Littleton, Colo., massacre would have been more grounded if the bigwig buck-passers had sat with me in Dennis Bobbitt's American government class at Washington High School. Bobbitt's summit occurred after the April 20 killings of 14 students and a teacher at Columbine High.

Bomb scares, guns at school, threats and hoaxes followed the national tragedy. I noted Bobbitt's seniors' comments in the aftermath with fascination.

Four years ago when I started studying with them in Alice Bennett's English classes, I wrote about some of the freshmen's rambunctious behavior. But those kids are adult upperclassmen now. They've grown to embrace the community's norms.

Witnessing the transformation has been one of the joys

of studying with the Class of 1999. Families, educators, coaches, businesses, churches and the community made it happen.

I've seen and written about the change as I've learned what it's like for teens and teachers today. It could've brought hope to Clinton's summit.

Courtney Bettis, who works at a day-care center, said some 5 and 6 year olds curse and hit others because they're taught that at home. She tries to teach them better behavior. Community service at an elementary school has shown Khaliah Sykes that by fourth grade, some kids are forced to raise themselves.

Jennifer Rogers shared a poem: "A child learns from what it lives."

Shanell Morrow said, "They weren't shown any love."

LeAnna Watson said the media keep bombarding children with tragedies: "The news is not for kids. I was asking my boyfriend, 'Is this the bad news channel?'"

Tim Adams said he liked a solution LeAnna offered—return prayer to public schools.

But I shared that prayer is mass-produced in some private schools over loudspeakers. It's disregarded, just as many public-address messages are from the Washington High principal's office.

Jennifer asked me, "So, is society as a whole in danger?"

I told her that what had happened at schools in Littleton and other places reminded me of full pots left cooking atop a high fire. Eventually, the contents boil, and some of the vital ingredients overflow into the flames.

Our society is boiling, and too many people on the edge are overflowing and taking others with them into the fire. We all must work to turn down the heat so the violence and hatred stop and everyone survives.

That reminded me of a chat I had with my friend Joanne Stallone. We oddly reasoned that not enough snow fell this year.

You see, people slow down when it snows. Mother Nature frees us from the rush of jobs, home and school, and our enslavement to beepers, cell phones, the media, computers and other so-called convenience items. Manners, courtesy, critical thinking, quiet time, prayer and kindness then return.

But we didn't get enough snow this year. We didn't slow down. The rush accelerated. Somehow, we must slow the march to hatred and violence.

We must create quiet time and moments for thinking and kindness for ourselves and especially for our young people, so they can grow up unafraid in places like Washington High School.

Take the time to be involved with and supportive of our teachers as they carry out their difficult mission, to work with our kids in school and at home as they struggle and succeed—that is the most important message that I took with me upon coming to the end of my tenure at Washington High School. Going into the final year of the project, I realized I owed the students, the educators and the community a great debt for enabling me to learn this important lesson as I discovered their many stories and shared them with others. That notion was captured in the column, **"Repaying a debt to Class of '99."** Reparations were in order. It also became an unexpected means of engaging the community to get involved in an urban school and in the lives of urban kids in ways that no one had ever thought possible.

My Aunt Juliet mailed a special package to me. "It's a little early for you to receive this token graduation gift for being in the Class of '99 at Washington High School," she wrote. "However, when I saw all of the things that are out for the Classes of '99 everywhere I just couldn't resist."

One gift was a stack of stickers. Many said "Good

Times," "Smiles," "Friends" and "Dreams." Another was a Hallmark Cards autograph book. A big "'99" is in the center of a huge bull's eye on the cover ringed by the words: Class of '99. We saved the best for last.

These were unexpected benefits from my studies with the Class of 1999 at Washington High School. Gutsy educators, other school officials and students have fed my curiosity and helped me journey toward a deeper understanding of our schools.

It's payback time now.

In June, a month before Juliet's gifts arrived, I told Bennett during our summer luncheon that year that I planned to donate $500 for a new college fund just for the Class of 1999 at Washington High School. It was my way of saying thank you to the students, teachers, school, district and community for letting me into their lives.

The challenges, dreams, tragedies and triumphs of students and how teachers get teens to learn have given readers of *The Star* new hope for public education. They've said it in hundreds of calls and in correspondence that's now nearly a foot high.

These inside-the-classroom columns have made Washington High a microcosm for adults who yearn to know what's up day to day in our schools and whether learning takes place as it did in their school days.

That has prompted a lot of folks to turn this new scholarship fund into a community project.

M. Craig Gaffney, president of the Wyandotte County Banking Center of UMB Bank, helped set up the Washington High School Class of 1999 Thank You Grant Fund. A retired university professor insisted on donating $150 after I told him of the new account.

UMB Vice President John P. Richardson, a Washington High graduate, also donated $50. A couple in Independence donated $350, boosting the balance to $1,050.

Some Washington High teachers have stopped me in the hall to ask how they could make donations, and so have others as word keeps getting around.

As the account grows, so will college opportunities for more students in the Class of '99. That's a fitting end-of-the-century graduation gift for the students, teachers and community of Washington High.

The fund ultimately grew to about $3,100 donated by people who were investing in the students' future. Alice Bennett put together the five-page criteria for the scholarships and assembled the scholarship review committee made up of herself, Beatrice McKindra, Scott Milkowart and Dennis Bobbitt—the other teachers who had let me take seats in their classes. Selection of the winners was based on merit, two letters of recommendation and student essays on "How I Plan, as an Adult, to Utilize My Personal Strengths and Assets to the Betterment of My Community." Only the most committed students qualified for the awards.

The commitment promised by those 1999 graduates of Washington High School should serve as an example to the rest of us. That doesn't necessarily mean we need to travel outside of our neighborhood to interact with students, although such efforts should occur, too. I think what it means is we all have to play more active roles in the lives of students and in the successful operation of the schools in our communities. Ultimately, we should all live in service to the community. To me the community is the ultimate customer, and anyone who has ever worked in a business knows that the customer is always right. I want to urge everyone I can to start caring again for all of our children of many beautiful colors. We have to care until it hurts, and then we have to care a little more. We have to care until we get our second wind of caring, and then we have to care until we're running only on an endorphin high alone of caring. I don't think we have a choice but to extend that Herculean hand to others of different races, genders, generations and cultures and push people to expect more from life and to give back more than they received. I don't think we have a choice if we hope at all to rest comfortably knowing that we have handed off the responsibilities and concerns of our community to a new generation well-trained and able to compete in the global market of the 21st century.

Part V
Epilogue:
Graduation and Beyond

raduation brought a natural end to the project. I had entered the skyscraper of public education at an urban
school and walked out with those students who also ex-
ited after 13 years in the nurturing societal structure. Actually
crossing the finish line left me feeling both exhilarated for having
kept my promise to readers of *The Kansas City Star* in going the
distance giving them a picture of what was going on day to day in
education, and sad because an investment of four years of my life
was coming to an end. But writing about the students' graduation
was not so much a sad occasion as one of great joy and anticipa-
tion for the future.

The graduation of the Class of 1999 was the culmination of a
long-term community investment in our kids. Their education is
supposed to be our community's investment in them, ensuring
they will either enter the workforce and be productive or go on to
college, grow and ultimately be successful. That financial and
social commitment from the community should be non-negotiable.
But in too many urban schools, that unwritten contract gets broken
early and often. I tried to bring out that students' expectations for
their own success are tied to the community's unfettered investment in them. That concept also is in a column, headlined
"Graduation time for the Class of '99."

Krista Cunningham took a break from her prom this
month to answer a few questions as president of the Class
of 1999 at Washington High School.

My previous attempts to interview her were unsuccess-
ful. Krista stays busy. The prom, with me in a tuxedo and
her in a beautiful gown, became our only opportunity to
talk.

These young adults now are pros at being interviewed. I
asked Krista what made her class exceptional.

"We're an independent class," she said. "We like to get stuff done by ourselves. "We're also not trying to be anybody that we're not. We're just ourselves."

Graduation is at 7 p.m. at Kansas City Kansas Community College. That's also where many of the 180 graduates, including Krista, will continue their education.

Krista has great expectations for tonight. "I hope our graduation will be really neat, outstanding, different from the rest!" she said.

As one of the speakers, I hope to do my part.

At the graduation I got to stand in a long, horseshoe-shaped receiving line with Washington High School faculty members. The line circled around the rows of chairs where the students would sit during the ceremony. It reminded me of the semi-circle drive in front of Washington High School, where I had for years seen big yellow school buses, parents, friends and siblings with cars drop off students at the main brick building. People pulled into the drive and went counterclockwise toward the front doors of the school building. In the graduation semi-circle the students marched in a clockwise direction on the hardwood floor of the gymnasium while their parents, other family members and friends watched and cheered from seats in the bleachers. The students at last had closed the circle in which we had begun our journey of learning together.

The students entered the gym in single file in their caps, gowns and handsome suits. Many of them gave great hugs of joy and thanks to the faculty members and to me or they at least shook hands with each of us. It was a moving procession.

During the speech that I had been asked to give, and that I wrote about in the column mentioned above, I pointed to a few gifts that I never expected to grow from my studies with the Class of 1999:

One gift is the scholarship fund I started with $500 to thank the students, faculty and community. Donations have come from as far away as Arizona and the fund was boosted by many contributions from the community and a $500 donation from *The Kansas City Star.*

Based on promises in their applications for the scholarships, the recipients plan to give back to their community. The scholarship recipients are Devon Bell, Kresha Crift, David Gray Jr., William Hawkins and Melissa Nichols. I ended up handling the final paperwork and writing the check to the colleges that each attended. Devon went to Kansas State University. Kresha went to the rival University of Kansas under the watchful eye of one of my advisers on this project, Dr. Renate Mai-Dalton, in the business school. David Gray Jr., went to Kansas City Kansas Community College. So did Melissa Nichols. And William Hawkins enrolled at Kansas State University. A woman who called me recently said she was eager to add to the fund for the students because, "I feel like I know them."

The second gift is this: Never before has a class been chronicled as this one has, with nearly 100 columns stretched over four years.

The third gift is that the teens' respect and care for their community has elevated the image of Kansas City, Kan.

The fourth gift is that the students also have uplifted their generation and themselves. They're teenagers doing positive things, and they've helped give adolescents a voice.

The fifth gift is that because so many people have read of these students' joys, hopes, ambitions, challenges and triumphs, this area now has raised expectations of what these young adults can achieve.

The sixth gift has been that the students now proudly have high expectations for themselves.

The final gift was that an East Coast film production company, which noticed the columns on *The Star's* Web site, has been following the Class of 1999 at Washington High. It's now exploring the possibility of creating a TV series or movie based on the students' and teachers' stories.[*]

I concluded my speech repeating what my dad had told me after he had dropped me off in 1973 at the University of Missouri-Columbia when I started my freshman year of college to study to be a journalist: "Dad shook my hand and his last words before he drove off were, 'I am expecting great things from you.' I have to add that I am still trying to meet those great expectations. Ladies and gentlemen of the Class of 1999, I also am expecting great things from you now."

However I followed that optimism with a dose of reality and some of the trepidation I felt for what the students had ahead of them. I brought that forward in a column headlined **"Struggles still ahead for grads."**

Marcus Powers and I talked about his future recently while he prepared to show his student-to-student research project to some middle school kids.

He wants to go to Atlanta, find a place to live, a job and a college. We talked about the challenges, costs and consequences of parachuting in as a stranger in an unfamiliar town.

Listening and offering feedback to teens happens in the margins of other things. That's one of the lasting lessons I learned before Marcus and other seniors in the Class of 1999 graduated Tuesday from Washington High School.

I found that it was in the margins of class time, at students' jobs, sporting events and other activities, that young people are open to questions, praise and guidance.

Many just want an adult to listen in a nonjudgmental way and care. Tim Adams has shared his joy with me over winning several forensics competitions and nine scholarships.

---

[*] Author's update: The show was never made. It was a great idea, but proved not sexy enough for a television audience.

218

I told Eva Tilford, class valedictorian, that I had proudly cut out newspaper articles featuring her in the Alpha Kappa Alpha Debutante Ball when she received a $3,500 scholarship. I've kept articles of Khaliah Sykes and Dedra Poole in the Delta Sigma Theta Cotillion.

I've clipped a newspaper picture of Devon Bell and Sarah Finney with U.S. Rep. Dennis Moore in Washington. I've kept articles and pictures of Keasha Cannon and Steve Brown as Washington High basketball stars. I've also clipped fashion photos of LeAnna Watson.

I've saved clippings of William Hawkins and twins Marcus and Michael Harris as the schools' star wrestlers. Many others have excelled, too, and I saw them honored at an awards program last Friday and at Tuesday's graduation.

In all, I've never seen so many students stand out so much at Washington High. Principal Jim Tinsley told the graduation audience that collectively the class had racked up a quarter-million dollars in scholarships.

But I now worry about what's to come for some of them. In the last two years, I've asked many students about their ACT and SAT scores.

I've been surprised that some of the best "A" students have earned only average marks on college entrance exams. I've shared my concerns with educators at the University of Kansas and the University of Missouri-Kansas City and with Ewing Marion Kauffman Foundation officials.

Low college entrance exam scores indicate years of educational neglect. Even top students get victimized by years of grade inflation and what Bennett in 1995 called "age promotion."

Students' diminished education devalues their "intellectual capital." (See Chapter 7.)

Compared with private and suburban students, urban teens often graduate at a competitive disadvantage.

They're set up to land in the intellectual ghettos and slums of backbreaking, low-paying, menial jobs.

But this class has as its motto "achieving victory through adversity." Bryan Rausch, in his graduation speech as a class salutatorian, quoted abolitionist Frederick Douglass, saying, "Where there is no struggle there is no progress."

In the margins I've told many of the teens that, like me, they'll have to struggle. But I expect many to succeed.

I have stayed in touch with many of the graduates through e-mail and get-togethers. They have kept me informed of their new experiences, their trials as well as their successes, hopes, plans and dreams. They still have great expectations for their own futures. That came out in a column I did headlined, **"Braving a new world."**

The holidays gave me a chance to send greeting cards, make phone calls and have lunch with graduates of the Class of 1999.

I've enjoyed our mini reunions. With some students it was as if we'd never parted after they'd graduated in May. We've stayed in touch via e-mail.

We'd spent so much time together.

Now they're teaching me about life after high school. Some, like Martin Bass, sat out college this semester to work and remain active in the community. College for Bass begins in the fall.

"After I do that then it's on to making a billion dollars," he said. "I have a clear vision of what I want to do—build up Kansas City, Kan., and put jobs back in place."

Unfortunately, his vision was interrupted after his family home and many others surrounding Washington High School were destroyed in a tornado on May 4, 2003.

Others, like Krista Cunningham, the Washington class president, are working and going to school. "I've been doing really well," said Cunningham, who is at Kansas City Kansas Community College pursuing a health-care career.

She loves the independence of college. "They don't tell you what to expect so you have to do your best to reach your goals," she said.

College has caused some students to adjust their sense of themselves and their expectations.

"I think we underestimated ourselves a lot," said Amber VonDerBruegge, who's studying financial advising at Kansas City Kansas Community College.

"I was expecting to struggle," said Jeanine Hegwood, who's at Langston University in Langston, Okla., with a Washington classmate, Nannette Young. Instead, each has been a standout student.

"College gave me a chance to get away from my parents and to put to work what they taught me," said Young, a biology major who's on the track team with Hegwood.

"I am so much better than what I thought," said VonDerBruegge, who's on her college volleyball team. "I feel a lot better about myself. I have a lot more self-esteem than what I had before."

Joseph Macklin, a business major at the University of Texas-San Antonio, credited Washington teachers for helping him succeed. "They kept me busy," said Macklin, who's playing college basketball.

Participating in college sports, however, is more demanding.

"While I was in high school, basketball was a hobby," said Macklin, who was a star on the Washington team. "But it's a job now."

The students also found that not everyone in college is focused on personal growth and academics. "You wouldn't

221

expect food fights in college," said Hegwood, who is president of her Langston class and is changing her major from physical therapy to international business.

"But it happened," Young said. So did dating problems, underage drinking, cliques, partying and juvenile pranks— just like high school.

College, however, can point young adults in new directions. Khaliah C. Sykes wanted to be a lawyer. Now she's a mortuary science student at Kansas City Kansas Community College.

Kresha Crift, a business administration and accounting major at the University of Kansas, said college is filled with adjustments. She's had to endure loud dormitories, relentless classwork demands and guys who won't grow up.

"I think they left their brains back in high school," Crift said.

"Some people act like they have no home training," said Natalie R. Washington, a music and liberal arts major at Xavier University in New Orleans. But she likes that warm urban church-oriented campus.

Washington urged high school students to get serious, pick a major and stick with it.

Sometimes, however, change is inevitable. William Hawkins, at Kansas State University, is shifting from premedicine to engineering. He's found that he likes engineering more.

Then there's Marcus Harris. He's committed to being an education major while playing football at St. Mary College in Leavenworth. His twin brother, Michael Harris, is a criminal law and justice student at Kansas City Kansas Community College.

Tim Adams, Washington Class of 1999 vice president, is majoring in theater and rhetoric communications at K-State. He's performed on campus and at the Apollo Theatre in Harlem.

He likes the diversity in experiences that college offers. He's learned to square dance, line dance and do the salsa.

"It's fun," he said. "College is what you make of it."

I couldn't agree more.

The contrast with high school seemed clear for some of the students. Kresha Crift said one of her biggest adjustments at the University of Kansas, where she was a business major, was that she was no longer a straight-A student. The workload and competition in college were far more intense. One of her instructors told me that Washington High School seemed to have sheltered the students, protecting them from the world that they eventually would have to face. I'd often see Kresha at KU during programs Renate Mai-Dalton had for her Multicultural Business Scholars program, which Kresha was in. But later I ran into Kresha at the University of Missouri-Kansas City, where she had transferred. Being closer to home won over being away at KU detached from her family and her community. She calls sometimes to update me on how well she is doing. We still laugh about her mother and my mother having the same birthday—May 14—though years separate them. And Kresha and I also share a July 17 birthday.

Still other students such as Eva Tilford did graduate from KU with a business degree. Tilford, who is part of Mai-Dalton's Multicultural Business Scholars Program, received a master's degree in accounting in May 2004, and in all likelihood became the first person in the Class of 1999 to get an advanced college diploma. But that's not surprising. Tilford was the Washington High School Class of 1999 valedictorian. Jeanine Hegwood after a long silence e-mailed me in 2003 with pictures of the man she had fallen in love with and news that she had started her own company of buying and rehabbing homes in Oklahoma City. Michael and Marcus Harris played football all four years at Washington High School. The twins, whom educators called the "dynamic duo," in April tried out and were picked for the 53-man roster of the Kansas City Shockers, a new, semi-professional football team based in Excelsior Springs, Mo. Financial problems had forced Michael Harris to leave Kansas City Kansas Community College, where he majored in secondary education, and Marcus Harris to not return to St. Mary College, where he played football and was an elementary education major. The Shockers, a North American Football League expansion team, has given the twins an opportunity for a second chance to play professional football, perhaps even for the Kansas City Chiefs. That remains their dream. And Jennifer Rogers' invitation for me to attend her wedding opened a new chapter for me with the students from Washington High School. She was the first person in the Class of 1999 who had invited me to see her walk down the aisle. I couldn't resist. I bought a card, added a check as a wedding gift and set off on U.S. 169 to Pittsburg, Kan., where she was in college at Pittsburg State University. I enjoyed updating people about Jennifer in the column, **"Wedding signals a sense of renewal."** The last I heard, she and her husband now have two children.

The 22-year-old woman in the beautiful white wedding gown entered the chapel at First Christian Church as Jennifer Rogers and left married to Chad Titterington.

I drove more than 200 miles round-trip this month to see the service and to ask one pivotal question to Jennifer: "Do you believe in God?" She quizzed me with it three years ago when I sat in the student desk behind her in Dennis Bobbitt's American government class for seniors.

I wrote about it in an April 17, 1999, column. (See Chapter 4.) It was among many deeply personal inquiries students made to help them make sense of tragic events in their lives.

Such questions were among the things I experienced.

Jennifer's question followed a fire that had left her and her family homeless and ruined many of their keepsakes. I told Jennifer then that faith sometimes is the only engine that powers people through such hardships.

I had not seen her since her graduation. She had enrolled at Pittsburg State University to study to be a teacher.

Like many of her classmates, she has used the Internet to remain in touch. Her e-mail last month invited me to her wedding.

She met the man of her dreams two years ago at a party when they both were students at Pittsburg State. Their love grew from that chance encounter.

"I'm so happy I'm speechless," said Chad, who now works full-time to support his new family.

Jennifer mailed me a formal invitation. Some of the Class of 1999 students have gotten married and have children.

But Jennifer was the first of the graduates to ask that I attend her wedding. When I got to know them they were ages 14 and 15. They're young adults now, taking on new responsibilities.

Jennifer smiled uncontrollably as her father, Phil Rogers, dressed in a tuxedo walked her down the aisle. Three bridesmaids in beautiful cream-colored gowns, three groomsmen and the groom—all in tuxedoes—waited with the Rev. Geoffrey Moran, who presided over the half-hour service.

It was a traditional wedding with about 70 people in the chapel. They beamed with pride, smiled and dabbed away tears during the faith-filled service.

"Life is a dance, and marriage is a choosing of partners for that dance," Moran said. He led the couple through vows of love and comfort in sickness and health and prayed for God to look with favor on the new union.

Let them "feel Your love holding them together in Jesus Christ's name" so they will grow as a family in peace.

"Love bears all they believe, all they hope, all they endure," Moran said. "Love never ends."

The couple exchanged rings. Moran asked God to strengthen the newlyweds, keep them faithful to each

225

other, fill them with joy and enable them to build a home together.

Phil and Sheri Rogers, Jennifer's parents, said faith, love and other people's help enabled them to rebuild their Kansas City, Kan., home so that it's better than it was before the fire. Faith enabled Jennifer to become only the second person in her family to graduate from high school and the first to go to college.

Faith, the Rogers said, is what keeps them happy. Jennifer and I hugged after the service, which was when I asked her the question she asked me in 1999: "Do you believe in God?"

"Oh yes," she said without hesitation. Her face radiated with joy and serenity on one of the happiest days of her life.

"I'm so excited," said Jennifer, who now is studying to be a social worker. She wants to help renew others' faith as people's assistance in her time of need benefited her.

It's the gift that keeps giving for those who believe.

The students are succeeding as adults, like everyone else, navigating the challenges in their own way and at their own pace. After graduation, the students' civic lessons got practical applications. My friends at Washington High School also became swept up in the historic Nov. 7, 2000, presidential election. Many of the Class of 1999 graduates were sophomores in college and now could vote in their first presidential election. That contest proved to be a monumental battle between Vice President Al Gore, a Democrat, and Texas Gov. George W. Bush. Florida, where Bush's brother, Jeb, was governor, proved to be the turnkey state in the election with counts and re-counts of many ballots and the whole thing going to the Supreme Court of the United States. The students I talked with took their right to vote seriously. I learned from them that their votes went to the different candidates. The column about this new adult responsibility ran under the headline **"Young, gifted and voting."**

The deafening political noise over Tuesday's elections made me nearly forget that the students in the Class of 1999 will get to vote in their first presidential race. I contacted some of them by phone or by e-mail.

They helped me recall things I had long forgotten.

I was in high school in 1971 when the 26th Amendment to the Constitution was ratified, lowering the voting age to 18. That action sprang from Vietnam War protests in which people said if Americans at age 18 were old enough to be drafted and die for their country, they were old enough to vote.

But I shared with the Washington High graduates that I didn't vote in the 1972 presidential contest in which GOP incumbent Richard Nixon defeated Democratic challenger George McGovern. I explained that although I am middle-age now, I was only 17 then.

I cast a ballot in my first presidential race in 1976 when Democratic challenger Jimmy Carter defeated Republican incumbent Gerald Ford. That was a cool experience, and I wanted to ensure that the students I'd gotten to know at Washington High School would enjoy similar memories in Tuesday's Oval Office contest of Democrat Al Gore vs. Republican George W. Bush.

But I realized from quizzing them on the election and sharing my experience that voting is a right that has to be taught. My mother took me and my three siblings to register to vote when we turned 18, and then she sent us absentee ballots for every election that occurred while we were in college.

Civil-rights activist Thomas Todd summed up my parents' view of voting in his speech last Saturday at the NAACP's 33rd Annual Freedom Fund Dinner in Kansas City. Its theme was "Race to Vote." People marched, cried and died so African-Americans could vote, Todd said.

"We need voter registration and voter participation," he said. "But we also need voter education. We must vote our own selfish enlightened interest and not just to keep somebody's job."

I was encouraged that nearly all of the Class of 1999 graduates I contacted were registered and planned to vote. Kresha Crift, a business major at the University of Kansas, was among them.

I connected Martin Bass in a conference call to the Kansas City, Kan., election office. He learned his registration is valid and where he must go to vote.

I had depended on my parents the way I had helped Bass. Other young people may need similar guidance.

But some don't. LeAnna Watson, a photography student at Central Missouri State University, registered on campus and is eager to vote. "I think it's our first chance to actually make a difference," she said.

La'Myka DeGraftenreed, an English and education major at Ottawa University, also registered on campus. "I feel that voting is a privilege that all people young or old should take advantage of," she said in an e-mail.

"We actually get to choose who is in charge of our nation, and lots of college kids couldn't care less," DeGraftenreed said. "That absolutely amazes me because as soon as something goes on that they don't agree with, they are quick to complain about it."

Nannette Young, also is charged up about voting. Young was getting her mother to send her an absentee ballot from home.

"I have been waiting for this moment since I turned 18," Young, a student at Langston University in Oklahoma, said in an e-mail. "I have always had an interest in politics, and I know that my vote will count for something."

Indeed. I let her and other Washington High graduates know that because this presidential race is incredibly close, it may rival the 1960 John F. Kennedy-Richard Nixon contest in which Kennedy won by a margin that amounted to one vote per precinct. That vote could be theirs.

Jeanine Hegwood, who's working while going to school at Rose State College in Oklahoma City, also is registered. Her e-mail included her election wishes.

She'd like a more popular voting system, which might include Internet ballots to excite people into participating in our democracy. She'd like the deception erased from the presidential debates and for them to include third-party candidates.

Maybe one day her election wishes will come true, giving us all better reasons to vote.

I hope I continue to hear from the students as long as I am at *The Kansas City Star* and as long as they know where to reach me. It's similar to when I was growing up as a kid in St. Louis. Often people would ring the doorbell to my dad's chemical company, and I'd learn from the happy voices that they were former students of Dad's or boys he had scooped off the inner-city streets surrounding his company. By exposing the youths to discipline with hard work, Dad had turned those misfits into men. Those folks still regularly troop by to renew ties with their former professor and the most demanding boss they had ever had. The same thing happens to me with students who have graduated from the Kansas City Association of Black Journalists urban journalism workshops, where I have served as an instructor since 1982. The students look me up saying they want demanding professionals like me to know how they have become successful, too. Sometimes they're seeking help on their journey toward that end.

But I've already learned that my investment and involvement in this project will never really end. Beverly McKain Jackson showed me that by inviting me to a reunion of her contemporaries of 1940s graduates of Washington High School. I wrote about their get-together and the possibilities it held for me in a column headlined **"Still classy, after all these years."** There among the "kids" in their 60s and 70s sat one of their teachers, Ruth Ann

Gatchell Eikermann:

"I was their teacher and their buddy," said Eikermann, who married the school football coach, Ed Eikermann. "There are family ties here. I know these people's parents."

Back then, the place was called Washington Rural High School in the Washington Rural School District, said Carroll Macke, Kansas City, Kan., School District spokesman.

The school opened in 1932 and was built to house 800 students. It became part of the Kansas City, Kan., district in 1967 as the city grew around it.

The monthly luncheons that Jackson organizes at Kelley's Grille & Bar in Basehor, Kan., sprang from the Class of 1947's 50th reunion, attended by more than 150 people last year. It included the other '40s graduates. "We enjoy each other more now than we did in high school," Jackson said. "We aren't worried about getting through high school, and we aren't worried about who's going with whom."

Jackson showed me a picture of the school. The circular drive wasn't there in her school days.

Neither were the additions that accommodated the baby boom. Enrollment swelled to more than 3,600 students in the early 1970s when the school had to resort to split shifts.

That's unimaginable compared to today's enrollment of 1,273 students or Jackson's class of 79 students in 1947 with a student body of just 320. Jackson said her class also had to endure World War II.

Jackson said some of her classmates quit school to fight for freedom abroad in that war. But people in the '40s classes don't reminisce about the war or the nation's troubled times when they get together.

Dick Richards, who played football for Washington Rural High, laughed with others about the first senior ditch day. They also joked about rides to school with Richards in a Model A Ford.

"We just always had a good time," Jodie Vose Porter said. "We never drank, and there were no drugs."

Dorthea "Dottie Diamond" Loehr added, "We had lots of good clean fun."

Gene Clark, who also played football, said: "These are my dearest friends. You'll never forget the people you went to high school with. Those to me were the best years of my life."

I can see that in my future. Because of Jackson, a retired schoolteacher, I know now that the ties the students in the Class of 1999 at Washington High School and I have forged will probably last a lifetime. Long after graduation, these kinds of "Kelley's" reunions will be my fate. I have told those students that I will always be happy to see them; I'll always be happy to help them if I can and if they have the wherewithal to reach out. I hope they will. What Gene Clark said, I think, was very true: "You'll never forget the people you went to high school with." His words echoed the thoughts that Krista Cunningham had shared with me just before graduation, that she and the other students planned to remain in touch. "I don't feel that high school ends people's friendships," Krista had told me. I know I for one will not forget those many inspiring, enthusiastic, committed young people and the lessons they and their hard-working teachers taught me over the four years that I "studied" with them—the four years that I walked in their shoes. I hope they keep that enthusiasm and as adults keep investing in each new generation of young people and in schools.

An African proverb says "Our world was not given to us by our parents but lent to us by our children." People who believe this as I do must do everything they can to give the world back to the children in better shape than they received it. That includes our schools. It's the only way education and our society will advance into the future.

Part VI
Closing Thoughts
by Alice Bennett

"Ouch" was my immediate reaction to re-reading my initial letters to Lewis, the letters I wrote to him in response to his column about a suburban teacher throwing in the towel. I found it difficult to re-read my harsh words after all these years. In fact, I still find it difficult to accept the tone of the letters. However, as a journalism teacher, I try to teach the power of words, and as an individual I have tried to live my life by "owning" my words. I am like Horton from the Dr. Seuss book, *Horton Lays an Egg*: "I said what I meant, and I meant what I said." So it is with the "letters." Yes, I wrote them. Yes, I was frustrated and angry. Yes, they are harsh and unforgiving. Yes, I believed in what I wrote. And while I flinch at the sting of my words, I do not apologize for writing them. I would not take them back. "I said what I meant, and I meant what I said"—then and now.

I suspect there will be readers who, after reviewing those letters, will condemn me as a person full of venom and hate and those same readers will probably wonder, "How could she possibly be a teacher?" Or, perhaps, they will say, "Boy, am I glad she's not my child's teacher!" I am positive many readers will wonder why I didn't just get out if I was so unhappy. I am sure there are others who will hold up my anger and harshness as an example of what is wrong with teachers, specifically, and with public education in general. Perhaps they are right.

I would like to think I possess one admirable trait that is usually attributed to teachers—that we are lifelong learners. For it is this attribute that probably best describes the experiences I have had and continue to have in my classroom and best describes my journey with Lewis.

Never in my wildest imagination did I ever think Lewis, or anyone else, would acknowledge or respond to my letters. Through the years, I have painfully learned the lesson that teachers' voices are ignored—ignored by building administrators, office staff, counselors, central office administrators and the school board. Through the years I have had to accept that, in the educational system, I am "just" a classroom teacher—"just" meaning bottom of the hierarchy—the least important. (It is my perception that the only time this practice changes is when an administrator, superintendent or the school board announces it wants teacher "input." Translate "input" to "buy in." They simply want your cooperation for a "done deal.")

Lewis, however, did respond. He met my frustration with soft-spoken curiosity and an invitation, an invitation to meet with him. It was an interesting meeting when I finally found the courage to travel to the building of *The Kansas City Star* and find his niche on the second floor. How patient he was as I tried to contain the tears. On the one hand, I was grateful that he was acknowledging my letters. On the other hand, I was flustered talking with a professional journalist face to face about the issues that were causing my anger. I was fearful of an unknown response from him. I am sure Lewis had questions from his colleagues regarding the woman who sat blubbering by his desk that afternoon. However, my tears have dried, and I have come to learn that Lewis doesn't place much importance on what his colleagues think.

The result of the meeting seemed simple enough. Lewis wanted to come visit my classroom. Would it be OK? I agreed. Would I make the arrangements and clear it with the proper personnel? I agreed. Only I didn't. I remember thinking: This will be a one-time visit. It will break up the grind for my students and me. To tell the truth, I don't remember much about Lewis' first visit. I don't remember that any earth-shattering lesson took place. I don't remember any light-bulb-coming-on-in-the-head moments with my students. I don't remember any embarrassing, horrendous outbursts taking place. However, something must have happened.

A few days later, Lewis called. He had a proposal. He wanted to do a series of columns. Could he visit my classes regularly? I agreed. Would I make the arrangements and clear it with the proper personnel? I agreed. Only, again, I didn't. I believed that, if I approached my principal, Lewis' vision and visits would lose their purity. His visits would become guided public relations fodder. After all, it's a principal's job to be sure the school doesn't get a bad rap. This is not a judgment against the individual who was my principal at the time. It was, continues to be, my perception of how the educational bureaucratic system works. Ironically, the columns that Lewis wrote during his four-year residency did indeed turn out to be good public relations—the kind of public relations that money just can't buy and politicians aspire to. He gave Washington High School a face and put us on the map. We were no longer just entries on the Kansas City, Kan., police blotter.

Lewis' columns took me out of obscurity and gave me some notoriety. Teachers at district in-service meetings would come up to me wanting to know whether I was "the" Alice Bennett in Lewis' columns. They were intrigued about how it all came about. They wanted to know whether my principal ever said anything about the columns. (No, he never did. Not once.) They wanted to know how the students acted when Lewis was there and what their response was to the columns. Did I ever hear from readers? The columns began appearing on a bulletin board at my church. Neighbors, friends and other building teachers would let me know I was in the paper again, just in case I happened to miss it. I have to admit, it was nice to be recognized and not patronized.

Career teachers learn to tolerate patronizing attitudes toward themselves and what they do. My students tell me that they would not "put up with" what I put up with. "You don't make enough money," they say. Colleagues in surrounding suburban districts tell me students tell them the same thing. In a society that worships a high salary, teachers are viewed as "chumps." (Can you say salary cap?) If the students don't say it, the look on their faces as they watch teachers struggle with disrespectful students, verbal abuse and disruptive behavior tells us that they pity us.

While I won't say it's true in other school districts (although I suspect it is), in my district it is my perception that we still have the "us" and "them" division. Teachers who have moved out and "up" from the classroom quickly distance themselves from those of us who have remained. It is more than an implication that those colleagues are now "better" than classroom teachers. They are. They meet our society's success standards—they earn more money and take less crap.

While I do not believe that teachers, or anyone else, should depend on the praise of others as the plumb line for doing a good job, we all like positive recognition and a pat on the back when it is meant with sincerity. Lewis was, and continues to be, sincere. Sharing my life and classroom with Lewis was a risk I never regretted. His columns became a mirror in which I could reflect why I wanted to be a teacher in the first place and remember there have been and continue to be some very good moments in my classroom.

Looking back on the experience, I remember my students being indifferent to Lewis at first. After all, they were freshmen and were preoccupied with things other than this immaculate man in a dark suit and black overcoat showing up once or twice a week. However, over time Lewis' visits just became part of the classroom, and students began to talk and share with him. I posted his columns in the room. Most of the students liked to read them.

Friendship, and notoriety, no matter how small, come with a price. The students Lewis had been following for four years would be graduating in just over a semester. Lewis called and wanted to meet. (Uh oh, another meeting.) The result of this meeting was simple enough. Lewis wanted to give back to the school and to the students. Would I help? I agreed. He was putting up $500 of his own money to start a scholarship fund and was soliciting money from others. Would I write the scholarship specifications, distribute the information to the students, gather the submissions and gather a panel of readers who would make the decision? I agreed. And I did. But what I also remember is this. After Lewis had spent four years of learning, sharing and writing about the students and their lives, they responded to his final commitment to them by not responding. One scholarship submission was received by the deadline. I had to "beat the bushes" to get more students to fill out a one-page data sheet and write a 250-word essay, then bring the two papers to my room. I extended the deadline three times! The panel finally chose the scholarship recipients, and Lewis' commitment to the students, which was unlike any I have ever seen in my career, came to a close.

I know that some of those students still keep in contact with Lewis. I know that two of the other three teachers who let Lewis come into their classrooms still have contact with him. Me? Well, he has been diligent in keeping our friendship intact, and I am grateful for that. Lewis may not have a lot to say to his colleagues, but he is committed to his community and his friends. And that is a good thing.

Lewis' visits and columns reinforced my personal pride in what I do and have reminded me to treat the hardness, verbal abuse and disrespect I face every day with kindness and respect. It took the eyes and curiosity of a stranger to bring those lessons to my heart.

Almost a decade has passed since I wrote my scathing letters. Would I write them again? I don't know. I am older and a lot more tired now. I have endured a lot of SOS. What I do know is that my frustration and the fire in my belly have not dissipated.

Unfortunately, the atrocities I was "screaming" about when Lewis contacted me haven't gone away. However, I'm still here in "my" school with "my" students, still trying to make sense of it all and to survive and to help my students survive. I am still in the classroom trying my best to prepare my students for a future that makes me fearful and is one that I barely can imagine. As a friend and colleague says, "You're still spitting in the wind."

To many of my students, education is not a priority, and they show up daily, and have for 25 years, without a pencil or paper or homework (which I don't assign anymore) or textbook or any interest in learning. I become, on a daily basis, a convenience store. Before readers assume that these students cannot afford these items, please be aware that at the close of school when the custodians go through the halls and open all the lockers to clean them out, there are hundreds of unused spiral notebooks and unopened packets of pencils that their mothers purchased for them.

My school implemented the use of uniforms a couple of years ago. As a result, I have had to become the "fashion patrol." (I say "have had to" because the building administration has told teachers in front of the students that if they enter a classroom and students are not dressed according to the policy, the teacher will be called out.)

Obviously, some days I get very discouraged. Other days I find a way to chuckle or am rewarded with some good writing from a student or see an improvement, at least for today, from a student who has been troublesome. On discouraging days, I sometimes think back to Lewis and his visits. I pull out an old column and remember that student or this incident and hope that either Lewis or I made a difference in that young person's life. Yes, I'm still "spitting in the wind." And, yes, I meant what I wrote "yesterday," and I mean what I write today.

Part VI
Closing Thoughts
by Dr. Ray Daniels, Superintendent
Kansas City, Kansas, Schools

Lewis Diuguid made a commitment in the mid-1990s to follow students at Washington High School in the Kansas City, Kan., School District through their four-year high school experience. The result was a series of columns that depicted the joys and frustrations of teachers and students in an urban high school.

Although I was not superintendent of schools at that time, I was an assistant superintendent and remember other educators saying the school district was "nuts" for allowing a columnist into a school. However, the gratifying result was the ability of Lewis' readers to understand the process of education in an urban community.

Lewis' perceptive insight into the educational process at Washington High School resulted in his unwavering vision to present the information in his columns in a way that was never unfair to students or teachers. He portrayed the good and the bad in the professional journalistic style that he is noted for.

The "look" inside an urban high school allowed others, both educators and the general public, to see the challenges that both students and teachers face every day. But the readers also rejoiced in the rewarding experience that successful students and teachers experienced in an urban school.

At about the same time that Lewis was taking a "hard look" at urban education, the school district was also taking a hard look at student achievement throughout the school district.

The school district's conclusion was that, although many students were doing well, changes needed to be made in order for all students to be successful academically.

An initiative, First Things First, was adopted as a vehicle to improve student achievement throughout the school district. Today the initiative is no longer a "reform effort"; it's just the way we do business.

The focus is on:
- Improving teaching and learning.
- Building relationships with parents and students.
- Continuous improvement in achievement scores.

Results have been gratifying:
- The achievement gap for minorities and students living in poverty is closing.
- More students are moving out of the lower performance categories of unsatisfactory and basic and into categories of proficient and above on student reading and math tests.
- Student attendance has improved.
- More students are graduating from high school.
- Fewer students are dropping out of school.

While the district is celebrating its successes, the effort will not be completed until all students are achieving at or above an education level of proficiency.

Just as Lewis' in-depth study of urban education highlighted his and the school district's ability to take a chance, the rewarding results of the district's chance to improve student achievement have made it a satisfying endeavor.

(Author's note: *The Kansas City Star* reported Aug. 25, 2004, that Ray Daniels, 62, was retiring at the end of the 2004-2005 school year.)

Works Cited

Chideya, Farai. *Don't Believe the Hype: Fighting Cultural Misinformation about African Americans.* New York: Penguin, 1995.

Court, Jamie. *Corporateering.* New York: Jeremy P. Tarcher/Putnam, 2003.

"Education secretary labels NEA as 'terrorist.'" *The Kansas City Star.* 24 February 2004: A-3.

Freire, Paulo. *Pedagogy of the Oppressed.* Trans. Myra Bergman Ramos. New York: Continuum, 2002.

Fried, SuEllen and Paula Fried, Ph.D., *Bullies, Targets & Witnesses: Helping Children Break the Pain Chain.* New York: M. Evans and Company, 2003.

Gil, Eliana, Ph.D. *United We Stand: A Book for People with Multiple Personalities.* Walnut Creek, CA: Launch Press, 1990.

Howard, Gary R. *We Can't Teach What We Don't Know: White Teachers, Multiracial Schools.* New York: Teachers College Press, 1999.

Hutcheson, Ron. "Students' names given to military. But parents can block Information." *The Kansas City Star.* 29 November 2002: A-1.

Institute for America's Future. "Memorandum to Education Reporters and Editorial Writers – Bush Administration 2005 Budget Fails Education." Common Dreams Progressive Newswire. 5 February 2004 <http://www.commondreams.org/cgi-bin/newsprint.cgi?file=/news2004/0205-09.htm>

240

McNally, Joel. "A Ghetto Within a Ghetto." Rethinking Schools Online. 10 June 2003. <http://www.rethinkingschools.org/archive/17_03/ghet173.shtml>

National Urban League. *State of Black America 2003*.

Potrikus, Alaina Sue. "Girls winning brain game." *The Kansas City Star*. 20 Sept. 2003: A-1.

Putnam, Robert D. *Bowling Alone: The Collapse and Revival of American Community*. New York: Simon & Schuster, 2000.

Robinson, Stephanie G. Personal Correspondence, 1995.

"The State of the News Media 2004." <http://www.stateofthenewsmedia.org/index.asp>

West, Cornell. Lannan Foundation, Santa Fe, New Mexico. 25 June 2003.

Zinn, Howard. *A People's History of the United States*. New York: HarperCollins, 1999.

Other titles mentioned in the book or suggested for further reading:

Bullard, Sara. *Free at Last: A History of the Civil Rights Movement and Those Who Died in the Struggle*. New York: Oxford University Press, 1993.

Fraser, George C. *Success Runs in Our Race*. New York: HarperCollins, 1996.

Shipler, David K. *A Country of Strangers: Blacks and Whites in America*. New York: Vintage Books, 1998.

Walsh, David. *Selling Out America's Children: How America Puts Profits Before Value – and What Parents Can Do*. Minneapolis: Fairview Press, 1995.

APPENDIX

"Wake up and read the graffiti"

July 28, 1996

On my morning jogs this month I watched workers build a concrete wall in Leawood to shield residents from traffic noise.

The workmen were methodical. So were the vandals who waited until the wall was done to scar it with gang graffiti.

Gangs and drugs are a part of life in Johnson County and other area suburbs. Bill Cross drove that point home this month to 150 teachers in his Ottawa University graduate class, Juvenile Gangs and Drugs: A Challenge to Education.

A third of the teachers were from Johnson County school districts. They were the largest group of educators from 31 school districts in the class.

"I don't think that I was aware until recently that some of the students were involved in gangs," said Robert Higgins, an American history and world geography teacher at Shawnee Mission Northwest High School.

Cross' class contained microbursts of information designed to help teachers reach troubled kids. The educators visited urban neighborhoods to learn about graffiti and gang signs that many admitted overlooking in their communities.

"Some saw the graffiti in the inner city and said, 'Oh my gosh! I've seen the same thing in Johnson County, in Clay County, in eastern Jackson County ... ,'" Cross said. "Or they couldn't understand why a person had red shoelaces on in a suburban school or a pant leg rolled up a bit."

He said a developing trend is that Kansas City gang members have become more covert because authorities know how to spot them. But in the suburbs and small towns, tagging and flashing are in the open because kids know that their communities are in denial.

More than a dozen guest lecturers exposed teachers to our world's underbelly.

Society is seeing more bizarre crimes stoked by drugs and alcohol, said Gary G. Forrest, a clinical psychologist and noted author from Colorado Springs, Colo. Television, movies and music have tainted the community well with antisocial problem-solving skills.

"The mode is the con—the person who can work less and be paid more," Forrest said. Often that lifestyle leads to crime, and people end up in prison.

The teachers toured the Lansing Correctional Facility, and the next day Lansing Warden David McKune and William J. Graff, Leavenworth Detention Center warden, were speakers in their class.

"The population is younger and more impulsive," McKune said. "Traditional types of management don't work.

"They just don't care about people, and they don't care about themselves."

The prisons are using new techniques. So are community rehab programs such as Jackson County's drug court, said Molly Merrigan, an assistant Jackson County prosecutor.

"The goal is to help folks alter their destructive lifestyles and make the community safer," she said. "I think the worst thing we can do is ignore the problem and think it will go away."

Other lecturers urged the teachers to be more creative.

"Our kids need to be counseled, and we can do that," said Gwen L. Stephenson-Murphy with ABC Educational Consultants. "You are the closest person to these kids. You are even closer than their parents."

Kansas City Police Officer Jennifer Wolf lifted the teachers' spirits, saying they needed more community and family support.

"You've made presidents," she said. "Just by you being here says you care about your kids."

If only more cared as much.

"Nurturing a feeling for history"

Nov. 11, 1997

Scott Milkowart's students did their reports and took tests on the 1950s. He then quickly marched them into the 1960s in his American history class at Washington High School.

History never seemed this interesting, this comprehensive or this real when I was in high school in the late '60s and early '70s. Like all good teachers, Milkowart's lectures enhance what his juniors are reading in their textbooks.

But he also rockets history into the students' high-tech world by showing videos on a VCR and CD-ROMs on his computer. Milkowart used CD-ROM technology to show some of President John F. Kennedy's speeches. Both Milkowart's computer and his VCR as electronic classroom aids were hooked to a big color TV on one mobile cart.

This imposing teaching assistant stands taller than Milkowart and has broader shoulders. Milkowart uses the multimedia setup to make history more vital and relevant to his students.

I've been fascinated by this technological spin in my third year of sitting with the Class of 1999 at Washington High in Kansas City, Kan. I've also discovered that the history they're learning is also more multicultural than what I was taught.

Milkowart is giving his students a more accurate picture of the many colors in the mosaic that we call America.

"I give my kids kind of what I missed," Milkowart said. "That way I'm learning right along with them."

In one class, the students watched the video "Eyes on the Prize," which focused on the civil rights movement. Milkowart also handed his kids a copy of an Alabama literacy test, which was used to keep black people from voting.

In the video, his students saw the marches, the brutality and the moving speeches by the Rev. Martin Luther King Jr., Malcolm X and President Lyndon B. Johnson.

246

I joined the discussion that followed, telling the students that television took the struggle for equality into people's homes. More than newspapers, magazines and radio, TV made the status quo of segregation, discrimination and racism something Americans no longer could ignore.

Students used the book, *Free at Last: A History of the Civil Rights Movement & Those Who Died in the Struggle*, and worked in groups on reports.

Steve Brown's group told us of the 1963 murder of Mississippi NAACP leader Medgar Evers. Milkowart updated the book, saying Byron De La Beckwith had gotten off in two earlier trials but was convicted in 1994 in the slaying.

The students knew the case from the movie "Ghosts of Mississippi." Amber Cantrell, Khisha Crosby and Krista Cunningham reported on bombings that killed adults and children in the civil rights movement.

"It's different when it kills children," Milkowart said. "It's hard, but it made their fight even stronger."

A week later and in a different class, Milkowart projected CD-ROM speeches by President John F. Kennedy on the TV. One was on the space race. In another Kennedy moved the nation by saying, "Ask not what your country can do for you; ask what you can do for your country."

Kennedy inspired Americans to fight injustice and aggression worldwide, Milkowart said. "The threat of communism was real and the threat of nuclear war was real," Milkowart said.

His classes also covered the Kennedy vs. Nixon election and their historic TV debates, the Bay of Pigs, the Cuban missile crisis, the duck-and-cover bomb drills that kids like me did in schools, the Soviets, Kennedy's assassination, the Warren Commission report and civil rights bills. A lot of memories came flooding back.

Milkowart let me share some of my recollections with his students. It felt good to help make history studies more vibrant than I ever dreamed possible.

"Pushy recruiters descend on high schools"

January 29, 2003

A disturbing drama unfolded in the lobby of my daughter's high school while I waited recently to pick up her and some of her friends.

A military recruiter in uniform stopped a teenage girl to talk about joining his branch of the service. She laughed and smiled but offered no commitment.

But the recruiter persisted until he got her to agree to see him later at his office. He said she would be sold on signing up when he finished explaining the benefits.

Since last year, the military's access to our kids got a lot easier. That's when Congress ordered school-to-military cooperation as part of the No Child Left Behind education overhaul that President Bush sought.

The law went into effect in July, requiring public and private high school administrators to let military recruiters onto campuses that receive money under the Elementary and Secondary Education Act. Only private schools with religious objections to military service are exempt.

Schools that refuse admittance to military recruiters could lose federal financing. That is not an attractive option for any school district in these tough economic times of program cuts, large class sizes and teacher shortages.

A joint letter from Defense Secretary Donald Rumsfeld and Education Secretary Rod Paige told schools to "work closely with military recruiters." The law requires that schools turn over the names, addresses and telephone numbers of juniors as well as graduating seniors.

It's also why military recruiters keep calling my home seeking to "sell" my daughters on the service. The only hope for kids is if parents tell school administrators not to surrender students' personal information to military officials. But I worry that this option will slip under many parents' protective radar screen.

The change in the law is taking place as the nation contends with the war on terrorism and as Bush builds up U.S. forces to invade Iraq. Signing up these days for service is different from the post-Vietnam War volunteer military.

The likelihood of being sent into combat was remote then. It's not now.

Conditions are almost as they were when I registered for the Selective Service in July 1973 at age 18. The end of the Vietnam War was two years into the future.

I like an idea Rep. Charles Rangel, a New York Democrat, is pushing in Congress. His proposal would reinstate the draft for the first time since 1973.

Rangel wants the draft returned to remove the anesthetic covering from today's war rhetoric. He wants everyone to sacrifice and know the horrors of war.

The public has largely been protected from it. News stories and footage of missile strikes have made war about as real to people as video games.

A real war should be borne by everyone rather than the military being filled with a disproportionate share of minorities and the poor. Some critics call the volunteer service a "poverty draft" because its specialized training, career opportunities and college possibilities attract people with few options.

I favor neither the draft nor military recruiters getting greater access to our children. Watching the fast-talking recruiter outclass that high school girl wasn't pretty. However, her promise to visit him later seemed empty, too.

But it showed me what's happening in our schools. I'd rather see dozens of college recruiters hanging out at every high school enticing students to sign up for universities.

I'd rather see recruiters discussing career options with students. I'd also prefer to see banks, credit unions and people with scholarship and grant applications milling about school lobbies providing young people with the financing they need to get to college and graduate with good jobs.

If those adults were as aggressive as the military recruiters, our kids would have a more peaceful and productive future. Our country would, too.

List of Columns
(in the order that they appear in the book)

Chapter 4

Part III (Portraits)

Chapter 5

March 17, 1998   "Parents: Fill those bleachers"

Chapter 6

April 10, 1999   "Lessons in music and life"
                        (Lindsey portrait)
Jan. 24, 1996   "When children graduate as
                        thinkers, we all reap the rewards"
Nov. 4, 1995   "Simple isn't the answer"
Jan. 8, 1997   "Employers will shun students who
                        shunned writing lessons"
May 8, 1996   "These days, making the grade in
                        school means smart timing"
April 10, 1996   "Teen generation's thoughts
                        developed with TV messages"
April 4, 1996   "Attacked from all sides"
June 7, 1997   "Media hype casts a spell over
                        youths"
Sept. 5, 1998   "Pressure, heat routine during
                        class"

Chapter 7

Dec. 14, 1996   "Teens thrive on spirit of discovery"
Dec. 9, 1997   "Listening to history sing loudly"
Nov. 14, 1998   "Hands-on history on a hike"
Oct. 21, 1997   "A real man can wear an apron"
Sept. 12, 1998   "Caught up in the flow of history"
Nov. 11, 1997   "Nurturing a feeling for history" (in
                        Appendix)
May 25, 1996   "Learning to confront prejudice"

Chapter 8

April 28, 1998   "Hugs are symbolic for teens"
                        (Jeffries/McLennan portrait)
April 27, 1999   "Celebrate to avoid disaster"
February 14, 1996   "The old challenge is with us still:
                        Triumph over mediocrity"
May 15, 1996   "Teenagers get a lesson in learning
                        as partners in education"

My thanks to The Kansas City Star *for allowing the use of the above columns. They can be found in their entirety at* **www.kansascity.com**.*.*

Lewis W. Diuguid is vice president for community resources at *The Kansas City Star*. He serves on the editorial board, writes two columns a week for the opinion section and is responsible for *The Star*'s philanthropic efforts in the community. Since 1995 he has co-chaired the diversity initiative at *The Star* and since 1993 has trained Star Co. staff in diversity workshops. A graduate of the University of Missouri-Columbia School of Journalism, he has worked as a reporter, photographer, copy editor, automotive editor, assistant bureau chief, bureau chief, assistant city editor, associate editor and columnist.

Printed in the United States
66216LVS00002B/298

9 781581 125191